The Open University
Business School

rspectives and practice

Managing people and organisations

To be used with Unit 2

MBA Programme

The Open University, Walton Hall, Milton Keynes MK7 6AA

First published 2010. Third edition 2012.

Edited, designed and typeset by The Open University

Printed in the United Kingdom by Hobbs the Printers Limited, Brunel Road, Totton, Hampshire SO40 3WX

ISBN 978 1 8487 3999 4

3.1

Contents

Introduction to *Managing people and organisations*

We live in a world in which almost all activity in any society takes place through people acting together. Most of us are employed by organisations or operate single or small businesses and receive an income in return for our contribution to the activity of that organisation. It is important therefore to understand how organisations operate and why they are structured in the ways in which they are.

All organisations need to do several things in relation to the people of which they are composed. Organisations need to select, develop and reward their people; to structure and design their work; to resolve political conflicts; to lay down guidelines for their managers; and to plan for the future. Pugh suggests that, 'If we are to gain an insight into, and perhaps some control over, our situation in these arrangements, we need to develop our understanding of how such organisations function and why the people within them behave as they do' (2007, p. xi). This is not a simple task, however, especially as the nature of managing and organising is undergoing considerable change and embracing new advances in ideas and technologies. New challenges arise as managers constantly attempt to adapt to new forms of managing and organising.

The structure of this book is therefore designed in such a way as to provide you with frameworks and ways of thinking that will enable you, as a manager, to question and challenge the way you think about the world within which you manage. We will be integrating conceptual knowledge about managing people and organisations with opportunities to develop practical skills that will help you as an employee and/or as a manager. Each chapter in this book covers a topic that contributes to your understanding of how people and organisations function so that you can become a better manager of yourself, other people, and organisations. The chapters will touch on different levels of analysis, such as understanding organisations in their entirety, understanding groups within organisations and understanding the individual within the group. These differing levels of analysis offer a comprehensive study of organisational life.

You should test your understanding of the concepts that are introduced by examining your working life. This could involve analysing your actions, the actions of others, processes that occur within your organisation and/or key organisational events. The following is a list of recommended questions for you to use throughout the book as a means of evaluating the ideas, concepts and frameworks that are introduced:

- How useful is this for me?
- How can I modify this idea in light of my own experiences?
- Which theories do I think have the most validity in my organisation?
- Which do I think are most valid as applied across a range of organisations?

So, throughout this unit you are encouraged to relate the concepts and frameworks to your experience or your organisational setting. This constant reflective process makes this book a personal learning journey as it seeks to link academic and practitioner knowledge to your work practice.

Overall, your objectives for working through this book should be:

- to value your own knowledge and its contribution to understanding how to manage people and organisations
- to connect the study of management and organisations to your everyday experience
- to develop your knowledge about frameworks and models that describe organisational life in order to help you understand the effect of your behaviour at work, and the behaviour of those around you
- to learn about how organisations function so that you become a better manager of yourself, of other people and of organisations
- to achieve a reflective understanding of your own and others' theories and practices, which resonate with real-world situations and reveal complexities, messiness and tensions.

This unit covers the following topics.

Organisational context

This first section of Chapter 1 examines how organisations are structured and considers factors that shape organisations and create the 'uniqueness' of the organisation. It considers how well or poorly all the individual and interpersonal elements of the organisation fit together and what management challenges different organisational contexts may pose.

Organisational culture

The second section of Chapter 1 explores what is meant by culture, and establishes the importance of understanding your cultural context. It introduces established frameworks for classifying cultures and explores how you can read an organisation's culture by observing its physical settings and rituals and asking questions about the underlying assumptions and values these imply.

Understanding motivation

The concept of motivation is vital to all organisations and, hence, to their managers. The first section of Chapter 2 introduces theories of motivation and demonstrates how these can be helpful to managers in achieving greater understanding of the factors that influence employees' and managers' motivation at work.

Teams and groups

The second section of Chapter 2 considers the dynamics of the groups and teams you work in and how you relate to and work with others in those groups. The section aims to understand why team and group working is complex and complicated. You will critically evaluate different explanations of team and group work and also assess the role and nature of teams in contemporary organisations.

Managing people

Chapter 3, 'Managing people', is divided into four sections. The first looks at the development of human resource management and how it has emerged as a distinct approach to people management. The second, 'Organisational entry', looks at how contemporary employment relationships take many forms. The third, 'Performance and rewards', is concerned with evaluating employees as individuals in terms of their job performance. This process requires a quality of judgement that places a considerable responsibility on managers. The fourth section of Chapter 3, 'Developing human resources', considers how employees become effective in their jobs through the development of their skills, knowledge and attitudes in ways that benefit both the organisation and themselves. Managers, therefore, play crucial roles in purposefully structuring learning opportunities for employees.

These topics taken as a whole provide you with a framework that defines the core functional activities of managing people. Managers are required to understand the importance of good managerial practices and to make the best use of people. In Chapter 3 we pay particular attention to the concept of human resource management (HRM) and how this is seen to foster good human relationships in organisations, as well as striving to improve the efficiency of staff and their commitment to the objectives of the organisation.

1: Understanding organisations
Introduction

In this chapter you are going to be introduced to studying *organisational context* and *organisational culture.* We start with organisational context, exploring the make-up of organisations and how organisations have tried to set themselves up through dividing work into specific tasks and allocating roles and functions to enable the achievement of organisational goals. The constant search to find the right organisational arrangement has been an active area of study for organisation and management research. The section on organisational culture will try to encapsulate what an organisation is 'really like' through the examination of various frameworks and concepts. This should help you to understand your own and other organisations and also begin to see why organisational culture has become an exciting area of interest for managers.

1.1: Organisational context

No one can avoid experiencing organisations. From the moment we are born and until we die our lives are governed and constrained by organisations, and almost everyone works in an organisation at some point, albeit some are very small and some very large. However, even if you operate a single-person small business, you will still be part of a larger organisational network of suppliers and customers.

Although we have this all-pervading organisational experience, not very many people think deeply about how the organisational environment of work shapes and constrains the issues managers have to address. The **metaphors** we adopt in thinking about organisations shape the way we conceptualise the whole managerial endeavour. The dominant metaphor for organisations is of the organisation as a machine. This is a very powerful metaphor that we will explore in this chapter. This metaphor defines the central problem facing managers in organisations as one of control: controlling relationships with the external environments, such as markets or political policies, to ensure that the organisation achieves profits, or internally, ensuring that the people employed work to achieve the organisation's mission.

You will discover as you explore the material in the first section that controlling the way the organisation works is not an easily achieved objective. Indeed, the problem of how to get workers to do what managers require is one that has vexed both academics and practitioners ever since the Industrial Revolution in the eighteenth century created factories that separated home from work. It is a problem that still concerns managers today as we talk of performance management and focus on outcomes and rewarding achievement.

Domestic working

Inside a Nokia factory

However, this is not the only metaphor to describe organisations, and the first section will also explore alternative metaphors – particularly those of Gareth Morgan, who has written extensively on this topic. You will consider some of Morgan's ideas about organisations to help you 'read' your own organisation more effectively and therefore understand it better.

In this section you will:

- explore a number of theories and concepts about organisations and relate these to your own experience
- examine issues about how organisations are structured and the consequences of this
- identify and consider the factors that shape organisations and create the 'uniqueness' of the organisation.

What is an organisation?

Stop and reflect

Think about an organisation with which you are familiar. What are the features that make you call it an organisation? If someone interested in your organisation was visiting it tomorrow – what would you show them? Would someone in a different role than yours show people the same things?

Unless your organisation is very small, we suspect that you would find this quite challenging. If you work in an organisation that has separate departments then perhaps you notice that as a manager you may relate to the other departments but your workers often do not relate to them in the same way. Similarly, if your organisation has operations across the country or internationally, then these problems of what *is* the organisation become even more pronounced. Where do you stop? Equally, it may be that your organisation is part of a network of organisations seeking to achieve similar ends. This is particularly common in non-profit organisations working with government and inter-governmental organisations, for example. In such cases drawing the boundary between the internal and external environment may be problematic as well. Figure 1.1 shows some of the key elements of a distance learning university as an organisation (for example, The Open University in the UK), from the perspective of the Business School.

Even with this relatively oversimplified diagram (it does not show the wider aspects of the university, such as other faculties), you can see first of all that the university is complex, and that, depending on where someone sits in this environment, the organisation might look quite different. One feature of organisations is that they mean different things to different people even within the same organisation. The perspective of the individual defines her or his perspective on an organisation's identity and boundaries, and there are many such perspectives. The point here is that how we conventionally depict and describe the organisations we work for is just that – a convention – but that it has a very powerful and constraining hold on our thinking and stops us constructing our view of the organisation in different ways.

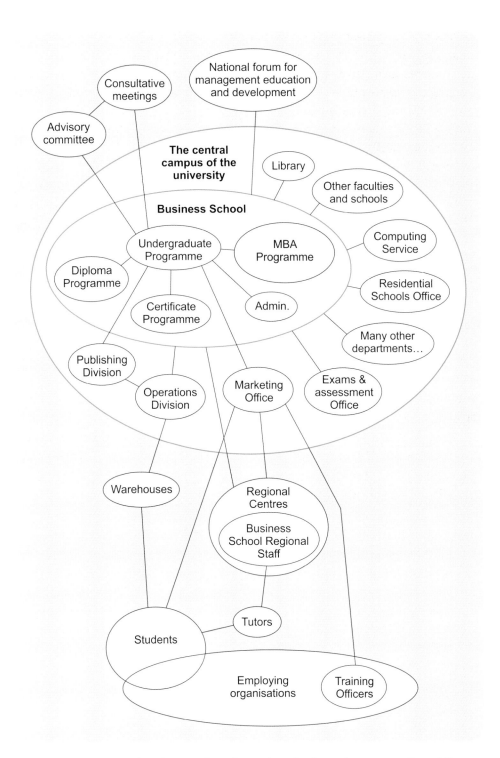

Figure 1.1: A view of a distance learning university from the perspective of the Business School

Organisations enable objectives to be achieved that could not be achieved by the efforts of individuals on their own. Organisations come in all shapes and sizes but have three factors in common: people, objectives and structure. It is the interaction of people to achieve objectives that forms the basis of an organisation, and some form of structure is needed within which people's interactions and efforts are focused. The direction and control of the interactions is the role of management. This sounds straightforward: organisations exist to achieve objectives and provide satisfaction to their members. However, we have already identified that those who come together to form organisations, those who work in them and those who manage them may have different objectives and needs, and different understandings of the organisation. There is a delicate balance to strike between coordinating activities in the most **rational** way and at the same time maintaining employees' and others' involvement and commitment to the organisation.

Some common features of organisations

Many of you will feel that the place in which you work is special. Yet, experience shows that managers in all sorts of organisations outline a very familiar range of management problems that are common. Thus, there is a paradox – each organisation is unique, but all organisations have much in common. All organisations are seeking to resolve a set of common problems: how to divide up the work and, at the same time, integrate it, and how to create a sense of identity.

Differentiation and integration

An organisation needs to find ways of dividing up the various tasks it must achieve in order to fulfil its main purposes without losing overall coordination and integration.

Differentiation is about this 'dividing up' in organisations; as a concept it works much as it does in biology. Single-celled species have no differentiation – or specialised organs – to perform particular tasks (although they still need to fulfil many of them, such as digestion and excretion). As animal species become more complex, they have to differentiate their cells to take on some specialist tasks. Some cells specialise and become the brain to deal with control and information, some form the blood to transmit nutrients around the organism, some form eyes to observe the environment, and so on. In organisations, a similar process occurs. As an organisation becomes more complex, one person can no longer carry out all the work, so there is a need to divide up tasks among people, and thus specialisms emerge. For example, a fashion manufacturer may require specialised sections to acquire resources, to transform inputs into output and to deliver these to customers, as well as people to manage these specialised sections.

However, as organisations grow, it becomes harder for people in different specialised sections to keep in contact with one another. This creates pressure for integrative mechanisms, such as a senior management group or interdepartmental meetings to ensure that those in charge of distinct functions are aware of issues for and from other parts of the organisation. However, this in turn adds another layer of complexity to the organisation.

This theme of 'differentiation and integration' was developed by Lawrence and Lorsch (1967). Although their examples draw on manufacturing, similar issues arise in all kinds of organisations. They found that differences in the structures of successful firms in the food and plastics industries were related to the amount of differentiation required by the environments in which they operated. They posed the question: why do people seek to build organisations? The answer they reached was that organisations enable people to find better solutions to the challenges posed by their environment.

This answer led them to three conclusions about organisational behaviour:

- People have purposes or goals, not organisations.
- People have to come together to coordinate their different activities and thus create an organisation.
- The effectiveness of an organisation depends on how well people's needs are satisfied by their planned transactions with their particular environment.

As they grow, organisations develop specialised units to deal with segments of their external environment. This differentiation of function and task within an organisation will be matched by different priorities, values and structures in the different units. For instance, a research and development department may have a long-term horizon and a very informal structure, whereas a production department may be dealing with day-to-day problems in a more formal system.

These differentiated tasks and sections need to connect with one another. This is the required integration and it, too, is affected by the nature of the external conditions.

Lawrence and Lorsch found that the firms they studied differentiated their functions into sub-units that dealt with a market environment (the task of sales), a techno-economic environment (the task of manufacturing) and a scientific environment (the task of research and development). Their findings are described by Pugh and Hickson:

> The greater the degree of uncertainty within each sub-environment and the greater the diversity between them, the greater was the need of the firms to differentiate between their sub-units … in order to be effective in each sub-environment …
>
> But greater differentiation brings with it potential for increased interdepartmental conflict as the specialist groups develop their own ways of dealing with the particular uncertainties of their particular environment. These differences are not just minor variations in outlook but may involve fundamental ways of thinking and behaving. In the plastics industry a sales manager may be discussing a potential new product in terms of whether it will perform in the customers' machinery, whether they will pay the cost and whether it can be got on to the market in three months' time. The research scientist at the same meeting may be thinking about whether the molecular structure of the material could be changed without affecting its stability and whether doing this would open out a line of research for the next two years which would be more interesting than other projects. These two specialists not only think differently, they dress differently, they have different habits of punctuality and so on. It therefore becomes crucial that a highly differentiated firm should have appropriate methods of integration … to perform well in the environment.

(Pugh and Hickson, 2007, pp. 58–63)

Although people often imagine that their organisation would be more effective if only everyone else thought as they did, Lawrence and Lorsch's analysis suggests that quite the opposite is true. If everyone thought as the production staff (or the administrators, or the sales people) do, organisations would be thoroughly ineffective. They need to incorporate very different perspectives and concerns even if this causes integration problems. Some of the problems of integration in a hospital are illustrated in the following example.

A case for more integration

After several months in his job as a junior hospital manager, Thomas began to see that how you viewed management processes very much depended on where you were working and for whom you were working. He had a friend who worked in one of the clinical departments looking after patients undergoing surgery. She saw things very differently. Whereas he was forever worrying about balancing the books, she thought much more about how her own department could get a larger slice of the cake. It did not seem to matter to her that others would have to make do with less. All she was concerned about was getting more for her own patients. Thomas felt she was taking the side of the clinicians, who did not seem to accept that they were part of a larger organisation. Then there were departments like Pathology, who just did everything their own way – well, he supposed they were the experts in their own field – but they did not seem to have much of a service ethos. Not like his department, which managed all the facilities – although you would think they never got anything right, judging by some of the complaints from the wards. The trouble was the ward managers had no idea about his own priorities.

Larger slice of the cake
To get a larger share (than others) of rewards, profits, resources, etc.

Such variety – such differentiation – does not apply only to large organisations (although the problems are usually more obvious in them). In a small project of two or three people trying to work cooperatively, tensions and arguments may arise not so much from poor personal relationships as from the need to cope with conflicting environmental demands and pressures. In larger organisations these tensions would be experienced more impersonally, in interdepartmental or policy arguments, but the origin is the same in both cases.

The challenge facing organisations, therefore, is how to achieve integration in an increasingly differentiated environment. One response has been the de-layering of management and the creation of self-managing teams. For example, in a large organisation catering may be done by a sub-contractor who is responsible for ensuring that a quality product is delivered. Thus, the parent organisation is relieved of the need to manage that process. In a manufacturing concern, small teams may be made responsible for producing a whole product rather than having a production line with all its attendant management problems. This approach has the merit of implying that integration in organisations is not simply a matter of structure but in fact a responsibility of everyone in the organisation.

Purpose and identity

All organisations have a purpose and an identity, and there are stereotypical views of how these differ. Commercial organisations are frequently held up by some as models of efficiency and effectiveness and by others as uncaring and unstable. Public sector organisations may be depicted as hidebound and unwilling to change, or as havens of altruism. Voluntary organisations can be considered amateur – or innovative and more responsive. In truth, there is often as much variation between organisations within each sector as there is between sectors. There are also sectors within sectors. Financial services seem to have an ethos quite different from that of the manufacturing industry. Housing associations are different from counselling organisations.

Hidebound
Unwilling or unable to change due to tradition or convention

Paton (1991) suggests that differences between sectors arise from the logic on which they are based:

Altruism
Selfless concern for the wellbeing of others

- Commercial organisations are based on a logic of profit, which implies notions of competitive positioning, measurable targets, the division of labour, optimisation, performance-related remuneration, and so on.

- Public sector organisations are based on a logic of accountability, which rests on concepts of service, impartiality, strict hierarchical control, universality, and the like.

- The social economy or third sector is based on a logic of commitment, in which people 'do what needs to be done' and are strongly influenced by shared values.

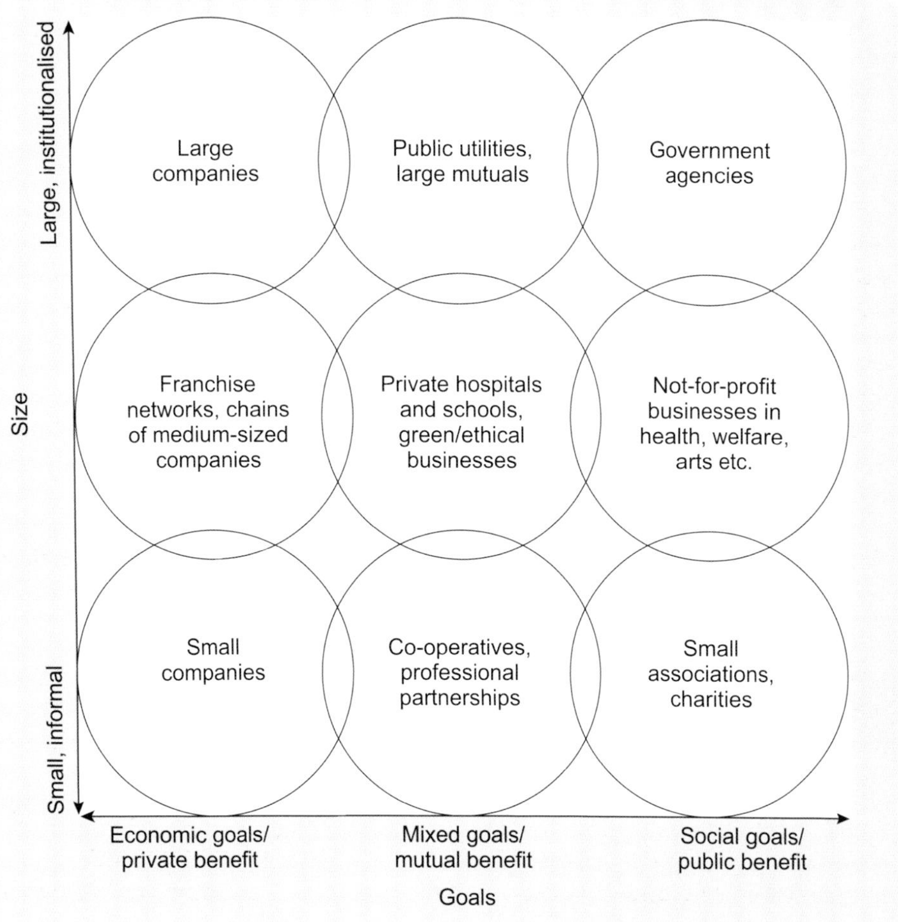

Figure 1.2: Organisations *circa* 1990, highlighting their diversity

This traditional view of sectoral differences is illustrated in Figure 1.2. However, the distinctions between public and private sectors have become blurred. Even organisations that regard themselves as clearly part of the public or voluntary sector will experience a pull towards other parts of the organisational economy. Organisations working in the field of residential care for the elderly, for example, have much in common regardless of whether they are commercial or non-profit providers. Local governments in the UK and elsewhere have lost some of their service provision responsibilities and are frequently purchasers of services from a wide range of commercial and non-profit organisations. In other words, many public bodies have been reconstituted and their goals redefined in more commercial terms. In parallel, many commercial organisations are recognising a range of concerns broader than delivering a profit to shareholders. Environmental and ethical concerns have risen up the business agenda. The whole organisational landscape is becoming more diverse and more complex. This blurring of boundaries is illustrated in Figure 1.3.

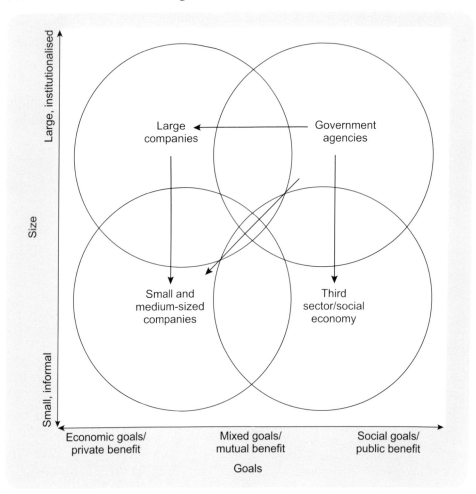

Figure 1.3: Organisations *circa* 2010, highlighting movement and overlap between sector boundaries

Organisational purposes are achieved by means of the organisation adopting a strategic orientation to the outside world. Organisations may adopt competitive or collaborative strategies, or a mixture of the two. Recently there has been greater stress on collaborative working for many organisations, which is linked to the concept of the network organisation. This type of organisation has taken the process of de-differentiation to its ultimate conclusion. Instead of differentiated functional departments bound together in one organisation, it consists of a partnership of several organisations. Hatch (1997) describes the principles underpinning this approach, and the example that follows illustrates how it has been adopted by Benetton, an Italian clothing company.

> Networks seem most likely to form when organisations face rapid technological change, shortened product life cycles and fragmented specialised markets. In a network, necessary assets are distributed among several network partners in such a way that it is not a single organisation that produces products or services, but rather the network at large that is the producer or provider.
>
> A network can be the result of massive outsourcing or collaboration between small firms whose scale of operations would not allow them to compete in international markets by themselves. Outsourcing means that many of the activities of a once complex organisation are moved outside the organisation's boundary. Sometimes the suppliers will be spin-off units, with the original organisation retaining only those activities for which it has a particular competence. All other necessary activities are purchased from other organisations. When all the task activities are outsourced, you have a virtual organisation.
>
> (Hatch, 1997, p. 191)

The Benetton organisation

Benetton is rethinking its global network of suppliers and distributors and defying conventional wisdom in the process. Its efforts may prove to be a model for other companies with far-flung operations.

In the 1980s, while the provocative magazine and billboard advertisements of Italian clothing company Benetton caught the consumer's eye, the company's tremendous growth, outstanding financial performance and innovative strategies were captivating the press, scholars and practitioners around the world. For many years, it was the archetypal example of the network organization – that is, an organization based on outsourcing, subcontracting and, more generally, on relationships developed between a large company and several small producers and distributors, or both.

Several factors contributed – and, to some extent, continue to contribute – to Benetton's success. First is its innovative operations-management techniques, such as delayed dyeing. Benetton postpones garment dyeing for as long as possible so that decisions about colours can reflect market trends better (the *tinto-in-capo* strategy). Second is its network organization for manufacturing. A network of subcontractors (mainly small and midsize enterprises, many of which are owned, completely or partly, by former or current Benetton employees) supply Benetton's factories. That structure has lowered Benetton's manufacturing and labour costs, has reduced its risk (which shifts to its suppliers) and has given it unbeatable flexibility. Third is the network organization for distribution: Benetton sells and distributes its products through agents, each responsible for developing a given market area. Benetton does not own the stores; its agents set up a contract relationship (a licensing agreement similar to a franchise) with the owners, who then sell Benetton products. Benetton supports the retailers with services such as merchandising.

To rest on one's laurels
To be satisfied with your achievements to date and not see the need for further improvement

But Benetton is not resting on its laurels. It is not waiting for a financial crisis or a performance slump to transform itself. True, overall performance has remained excellent ... Benetton's managers believe, however, that if the Treviso-based company is to remain competitive in the new global arena, it must have first-hand contact with the end customer, respond in real time to market changes and find new ways to ensure direct control over the supply chain.

To that end, the company is retaining its network structure but is changing the nature of the network. Whereas its main competitors have stuck with outsourcing, Benetton is gambling on vertical integration and centralization. It is betting – perhaps counter-intuitively – that it can remain flexible and achieve a high level of performance with a more complex network architecture in which it directly oversees key business processes throughout the supply chain. Benetton also is diversifying into sports – another move not entirely in keeping with conventional wisdom, which suggests companies should focus on their core businesses. The company's choice shows, however, that an enterprise can adapt its knowledge and competencies to a different, though closely related, industry. Finally, although it has embraced globalization, Benetton believes that sustainable value creation cannot be built merely by exploiting cost differentials between nations. It is committed to maintaining key functions at its base in industrialized northeastern Italy; even in its overseas locations, it has established production practices based on its Italian model. The aim is to achieve overseas profits not just from cheap labour, but from sound systems.

(Camuffo et al. 2001, pp. 46–52)

Many organisations work collaboratively without becoming network or virtual organisations. Partnership is in vogue within and between all sectors, making life even more complex for managers. One major problem that emerges from collaborative strategies can be a loss of autonomy for individual organisations. Agreements have to be reached with other organisations about the goals and methods to pursue. These negotiations can add to the complexity of the management task. There can also be tensions about organisational identity if smaller and less powerful organisations feel swamped by larger participants in their network.

Stop and reflect

Locate your organisation in Figure 1.3.

Identify any movements or overlaps between sector boundaries that have affected your organisation.

You may have found that your organisation sits clearly in one of the sectors, or, more likely, you may have found that it sits in some kind of intermediate position, operating for commercial purposes, but anxious to satisfy other agendas, such as accountability to a wider public. For example, there has been an increase in ethical investment companies. These have to operate according to the logic of profit (or cease to exist), but they also have pressures arising from their accountability for their investment decisions. Or your organisation may be in the social care sector: keen to provide an excellent service to people in your locality, but also having to operate on commercial principles when managing costs or face the loss of this service to a more cost-effective provider.

Size and life cycle

Most people would agree that an organisation's size fundamentally affects how it operates and what it is like as a place of work. In small organisations informality often rules. There is little division of labour and few rules and regulations. There is frequently a sense that procedures for budgeting and managing performance are made up in an ad hoc way, and there is little specialisation at either the professional or the administrative level. Often the manager has a multiplicity of roles and essentially has to do everything that is not in anyone else's job description (if such a thing exists!). In contrast, larger organisations typically feature an extensive division of labour, large professional staffs, numerous rules, regulations and internal systems for control, rewards and innovation.

Size is to some extent a function of the age of an organisation. Work by Daft (2000) suggested that there are four stages in an organisational life cycle: birth, youth, midlife and maturity.

At birth an organisation is entrepreneurial, often having a founder with a strong sense of ownership, who may find it difficult to delegate tasks to others. The organisation will probably be small, with processes of integration depending as much on force of personality as on any formal system.

In its youth stage the organisation and the number of employees grow. The owner has to delegate some authority to others (although there may be an inner circle of trusted colleagues). Formalisation of systems and procedures starts to emerge and so does the division of labour.

At midlife the organisation may be quite large, more formal in its systems and division of labour, and have manuals of procedures and agreed policies. There will be more support staff and problems of integration. There may be some loss of flexibility and creative capacity.

In maturity the organisation may be set in its ways, with large systems and procedures in place, and it may be in danger of stagnation. Decision making may be slow and centralised, and special task forces or teams may be required to overcome any obstacles. There may also be discussions about downsizing.

Few organisations follow this pattern exactly, but you may be able to identify, for example, restructuring programmes in your organisation that are symptomatic of moves between these stages.

Stop and reflect

At what stage in the life cycle is your organisation? What impact does this have on your job?

Up to this point, some of the factors that shape organisations have been highlighted, but even though this illustrates quite a lot of complexity and some sources of difference – it is only part of the picture. As indicated at the beginning, even given these factors, people in the same organisation will still argue about what the organisation is like and why it exists. The other key influences that shape thinking about organisations are the ideas we have about organisations and the way we conceptualise them.

The problem of rationality and control

> One of the most basic problems of modern management is that the mechanical way of thinking is so ingrained in our everyday conceptions of organization that it is often difficult to organize in any other way.
>
> (Morgan, 1986, p. 14)

So wrote **Gareth Morgan** in his book *Images of Organization*. In this book he sought to explain ways of understanding and thinking about organisations. He argued that by exploring different metaphors for organisations, managers could learn the art of reading and understanding them. The metaphors opened up new insights into the world of organisations. He developed several different metaphors to describe organisations: machines, organisms, brains, cultures, political systems, **psychic prisons**, flux and transformation, and instruments of domination.

The following box sets out the different concepts associated with each of Morgan's metaphors.

Archetypical metaphors for organisations (and associated concepts)

Machines

Efficiency, waste, maintenance, order, clockwork, cogs in a wheel, programmes, inputs and outputs, standardisation, production, measurement and control, design

Organisms

Living systems, environmental conditions, adaptation, life cycles, recycling, needs, **homeostasis**, evolution, survival of the fittest, health, illness

Brains

Learning, parallel information processing, distributed control, mindsets, intelligence, feedback, requisite variety, knowledge, networks

Cultures

Society, values, beliefs, laws, ideology, rituals, diversity, traditions, history, service, shared vision and mission, understanding, qualities, families

Political systems

Interests and rights, power, hidden agendas and backroom deals, authority, alliances, party-line, censorship, gatekeepers, leaders, conflict management

Psychic prisons

Conscious and unconscious processes, repression and regression, ego, denial, projection, coping and defence mechanisms, pain and pleasure principle, dysfunction, workaholism

Flux and transformation

Constant change, dynamic equilibrium, flow, self-organisation, systemic wisdom, attractors, chaos, complexity, butterfly effect, emergent properties, dialectics, paradox

Instruments of domination

Alienation, repression, imposing values, compliance, charisma, maintenance of power, force, exploitation, divide and rule, discrimination, corporate interest

(Source: Lawley, 2001)

We will now explore three of these metaphors and how they have shaped management thinking about organisations. The first and most pervasive is the notion of the organisation as being like a machine. The other two metaphors we explore are 'psychic prisons' and 'political systems'.

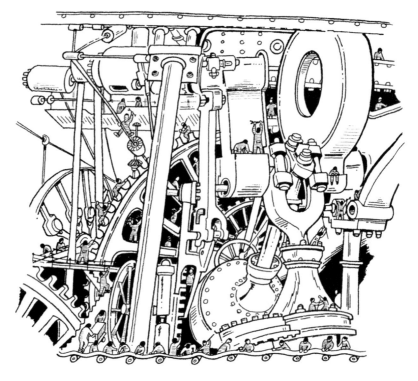

The organisation as a machine

Early thinking on business organisations assumed the economic model of rational persons purposively pursuing their ends or objectives. Max Weber (1864–1920), a German sociologist, described **bureaucracy** as the ultimate model of efficient organisation. He was concerned with the problem that still vexes managers about why people do as they are told. He saw this as stemming from some individuals having the power and authority to issue commands that are viewed as legitimate and therefore obeyed by others. We do not need at the moment to look at all three types of authority he identified (the others are traditional and charismatic authority), but we want to focus on the kind of authority that he saw as typifying modern society – legal-rational. The organisational form that flows from this is bureaucracy. Pugh and Hickson describe this in the following box.

Bureaucracy: the ultimate form of organisation

Weber's third type of authority system [is] the rational-legal one with its bureaucratic organizational form. This Weber sees as the dominant institution of modern society. The system is called rational because the means are expressly designed to achieve certain specific goals (i.e. the organization is like a well-designed machine with a certain function to perform, and every part of the machine contributes to the attainment of maximum performance of that function). It is legal because authority is exercised by means of a system of rules and procedures through the office which an individual occupies at a particular time. For such an organization Weber uses the name 'bureaucracy'. In common usage bureaucracy is synonymous with inefficiency, an emphasis on red tape and excessive writing and recording. Specifically it is identified with inefficient public administration. But in terms of his own definition, Weber states that a bureaucratic organization is technically the most efficient form of organization possible. 'Precision, speed, unambiguity, knowledge of files, continuity, discretion, unity, strict subordination, reduction of friction, and material and personal costs – these are raised to the optimum point in the strictly bureaucratic administration.' Weber himself uses the machine analogy when he says that the bureaucracy is like a modern machine, while other organizational forms are like non-mechanical methods of production.

The reason for the efficiency of the bureaucracy lies in its organizational form. As the means used are those which will best achieve the stated ends, it is unencumbered by the personal whims of the leader or by traditional procedures which are no longer applicable. This is because bureaucracies represent the final stage in depersonalisation. In such organizations there is a series of officials, whose roles are circumscribed by written definitions of their authority. These offices are arranged in a hierarchy, each successive step embracing all those beneath it. There is a set of rules and procedures within which every possible contingency is theoretically provided for. There is a 'bureau' for the safe keeping of all written records and files. It being an important part of the rationality of the system that information is written down. A clear separation is made between personal and business affairs, bolstered by a contractual method of appointment in terms of technical qualification for office. In such an organization authority is based in the office and commands are obeyed because the rules state that it is within the competence of a particular official to issue such commands. Also important is the stress on the appointment of experts. One of the signs of a developing bureaucracy is the growth of professional managers and an increase in the number of specialist experts with their own departments.

For Weber, this adds up to a highly efficient system of co-ordination and control. The rationality of the organization shows in the ability to 'calculate' the consequences of its actions. Because of the hierarchy of authority and the system of rules, control of the actions of individuals in the organization is assured; this is the depersonalization. Because of the employment of experts who have their specific areas of responsibility and the use of files, there is an amalgamation of the best available knowledge and a record of past behaviour of the organization. This enables predictions to be made about future events. The organization has rationality: 'the methodical attainment of a definitely given and practical end by means of an increasingly precise calculation of means'.

(Source: Pugh and Hickson, 2007, pp. 7–8)

In the 1880s an engineer called Frederick Taylor carried this rational approach to the logical conclusion and devised a way of analysing and synthesising work flows to achieve, as he saw it, the most effective ways of working. He observed people working, measured how long it took them to do tasks, and sought to devise the most efficient way of doing these tasks. This has sometimes been referred to as a 'time and motion' study.

With the invention of the conveyor belt, Henry Ford in particular carried this thinking forward. This view of control focused on extrinsic factors, using the conveyor belt to control the pace of work and offering high monetary rewards for tolerating this. This clearly increased the efficiency with which the workers produced cars but at a cost to social relations and job satisfaction. Charlie Chaplin's 1929 masterpiece *Modern Times* viciously satirised this approach to management, as illustrated in the film stills reproduced here.

Stills from *Modern Times* (1929)

Stop and reflect

We laugh today at the ludicrous situation Chaplin depicts, but it is worth reflecting on the extent to which these ideas still permeate the approach to modern management. To what extent is control and measurement of work a key feature of your work environment?

Organisations as psychic prisons

Although we emphasised in the introduction to this chapter that we construct our own images of organisations, Morgan argues that 'human beings have a knack for getting trapped in webs of their own creation' (Morgan, 2007, p. 207) and that because organisations are held together by people's ideas (conscious and unconscious) about what the organisation is, people find it hard to think of other ways of conceptualising how they might do things. They become prisoners of their own ideas. This is the second metaphor we explore.

Flexibility or the new Taylorism?

Call centres have been technology driven. They are the product of a combination of complex computerised systems, which allow the trained call-operator access to every customer's account and to every relevant element of the company's operations, and the automated call distribution system (ACD), which does away with the need for a switchboard and allows management to fully monitor and analyse every call. The technology, however, has produced some of the worst features of mass communication. Simon Roncoroni of L&R reported at a 1997 JPD conference that he has seen 'offices where individuals sit in tiny pig-pens with high screens round them, or in a long line as though they were in a factory'.

There are call centres which resemble the industrial sweatshops of the past, involving very cramped conditions for staff who work on their computers throughout their shift under very tightly controlled conditions. Those on specialised sales areas even have a script written for them so that it is easy to believe that their individuality is being negated. In many ways this is identical to the assembly line created by Ford engineers from the theories of Fredrick Taylor and parodied by Charlie Chaplin in the film *Modern Times*. It is as far removed from a flexible environment as you can get.

Lack of control over working time and methods is a great contributor to stress. It becomes, as Merilyn Armitage (1997) has called it, a 'psychic prison' from which inmates are tempted to use any device to escape, including continuing to speak to a caller who has long since hung up so no one else can get through. Absenteeism and sickness levels are notoriously high – one centre experienced a 20 per cent absence rate according to a survey carried out by the Merchants Group.

A further ratchet of control is secured by tying the pay system to an individual's performance, measured (so accurately) by the number of successful calls per hour. To complete the picture, the disciplinary system comes into force when a print-out shows that the employee does not appear to be earning his or her keep. There is some evidence of a rapid 'burn-out' after only 12 to 20 months' service (Welch, 1997); Vodafone's personnel manager is quoted in this article as expecting only a year's service from the typical applicant. A study of 106 units by the Merchants Group (*Personnel Today*, 1997) found that absenteeism averaged 4.8 per cent, compared with the CBI average figure of 3.7 for all employees. The report implied that a rate over 4 per cent indicated some kind of problem with stress, morale or integrity.

(Source: Stredwick and Ellis, 1998, pp. 166–7)

Stop and reflect

To what extent are these practices reflected in your own experience of work today?

To think outside of the box
To think differently from the established way or unconventionally

Morgan argues that this psychic prison metaphor is useful in encouraging people to think outside of the box – a phrase that in itself suggests a trap – and begin to think outside of the ideas that constrain them. Control may, in the call-centre, have become counter-productive, but people find it hard to think of ways of involving workers in the organisation other than by increasing control.

This feature of how the workers are monitored and controlled in both automated factories and call-centres was also explored by Michel Foucault (1979), a French philosopher and historian, who argued that surveillance and discipline of this kind was a central feature of the 'discourse' or frame of reference of management. By creating a discourse about how the organisation should operate, the powerful – i.e. managers – are able to control the workforce even when the latter think they are making their own choices about how they work. The following excerpt from Pugh and Hickson (2007) illustrates how Foucault saw power operating in the organisation.

The Foucault project that has had the biggest impact on organization theory is his analysis of power and authority in the organization. The organizations that he considers are those where the exercise of power in their everyday working is very visible (e.g., prisons, armies, hospitals, and schools). In these organizations, the warders, officers, doctors, and schoolmasters legitimately exercise considerable powers of discipline and control over the other members. His major work, *Discipline and Punish: The Birth of the Prison*, is a historical examination of the treatment of prisoners in the French penal system. … [H]e does not use the word *history* but rather *genealogy* to identify his analytical concerns. Genealogy is a 'form of history which can account for the constitution of knowledges, discourses and domains of objects.' …

It is the discourse or frame of reference of those involved that determines the way they think and act, and therefore how the organization and those in it function. The nature of the discourse explains the way in which organizations emerge, develop, and sustain themselves. …

Discourse, as Foucault formulates it, may be considered as the rules of the game for those in the organization. It is the way of thought that they take for granted. It shows not just in what they say, but also in the arrangements and technological devices that are used for control.

Here Foucault takes up the notion of the panopticon as designed by the early 19th-century British philosopher, Jeremy Bentham. Bentham developed a theoretical design for a prison building that allowed the warden to continually survey many prisoners, each in their own cell, while not being seen himself. Thus, the prisoners could not know whether they were being watched (hence *panopticon*, or all-seeing machine). The aim, in addition to being a cost-effective, low-staffed prison, was to instill correct behavior into the prisoners. Because they cannot know if they were being watched, they have to act properly all the time and so they internalize the rules. In Foucault's terms, the physical setting is thus part of the discourse.

In organizational life, what is considered as true are not objective facts but what is part of the discourse. For example, it may have been established that managerial work is worth more and should be paid more than physical work, and this is accepted without question. But only certain facts are regarded as knowledge, whereas other facts are omitted. In a discussion about the closure of a plant, for example, the profitable operation of the company will be taken to be part of the discourse. But the consequent economic and psychological disruption to redundant long-serving workers may not be included in the discourse, being deemed irrelevant to the company's performance. Prohibitions on discourse by the powerful serve to order and control it against the resistances of the rest.

Surveillance and discipline are also crucial parts of the discourse by which the powerful establish their 'truth' in organizations. Writing in the 1970s, Foucault presciently focuses on surveillance as the key control process of the powerful, even before modern technological developments such as closed-circuit television (CCTV), email trails, and large-scale computer databases vastly increased the reach of this process. So, 'Is it surprising that prisons resemble factories, schools, barracks, hospitals, which all resemble prisons?'

The aim of the discourse is thus to establish what is taken to be 'normal' by all the participants. But Foucault does not regard this argument as meaning that the powerful in organizations can simply impose their domination on the powerless. Power is relational. The discourse is a battlefield in which the powerful fight for their conceptions of truth and the powerless have ways of resisting. It may be established that joining trades unions or going on strike are also normal parts of the discourse. ... For the powerful, of course, such resistance is itself a justification of the need for surveillance and discipline.

So the basic question that Foucauldian analysts ask is, What is the discourse and how is it being formed? Barbara Townley has applied this approach to human resource management. An employment contract must leave much of the relationship between the organization and the individual undetermined. It can specify the system of remuneration to be paid, but can be only very general about the commitment and effort required from an employee. How, then, is the discourse governing these to be established? Managements acquire knowledge about employees by the application of personality and aptitude tests, grading systems, incentive schemes, developmental appraisals, or training programs. The results of these procedures do not constitute objective facts that are value neutral. What they also do is give more information about the employee and thus increase the opportunities for classification, evaluation, and control by top management – while at the same time establishing in the discourse that this is a normal, acceptable way to proceed.

Similarly, the establishment of bureaucracies ... or the introduction of scientific management ... are not only, or primarily, for efficiency, as their proponents argue. Their aim is to obtain knowledge to enable the organizationally powerful to establish the discourse that normalizes their control. ... Foucault coined the term *governmentality* to mean the strategies both of the organizational governance of those at the top and the self-governance of those below. The aims of modern accounting and IT systems are, likewise, to establish governmentality by obtaining knowledge to make the managers in the organization more open to both higher control and self-control.

(Source: Pugh and Hickson, 2007, pp. 112–14)

Foucault's point about the 'panoptic prison' is that surveillance is covert and the fact that the prisoners do not know whether they are being watched is what imposes 'self-discipline'. Although nowadays many management thinkers argue that the approach to controlling what people do is more people-centred, whether following the human relations school and the **Hawthorne Effect** or by attempts to manage organisational culture, others, such as Grey (2005), argue that surveillance still lies at the heart of the matter.

Stop and reflect

To what extent are modern techniques of surveillance used in workplaces today? What issues does this raise for you as a manager?

Pugh and Hickson mention the pervasiveness now of CCTV, email trails, databases and, in many organisations such as supermarkets, the use of mystery shoppers. Nowadays, if you are on an organisation's website, feedback will often be solicited to establish how happy you are with the service received. How often does your call to a supplier start with 'calls may be monitored for training purposes'? This raises ethical issues in the workplace – where does the boundary between what someone does at work and in their leisure time end for the employer. Many employees set up groups on Facebook or other social networking sites, and the downside is that some people have lost their jobs over comments made there about their employers. Some employers have CCTV in the office to deter minor thefts. There are no right answers to these questions, but they merit thought to understand what is ethical for you.

Organisations as political systems

This is the third of Morgan's metaphors that we will explore. It is concerned with issues of power, authority and superior/subordinate relationships, and here Morgan's metaphor is that of the ruler and ruled. Morgan sees that organisations are intensely political, with people plotting for advantage; however, this politicking at the same time is paradoxically 'undiscussable'. The very ideas presented earlier about organisations being rational entities work against openly acknowledging a conception of organisations as political arenas. Morgan argues that the organisation may be viewed as a mini-state with three potential sets of relationships between the individual and the organisation: unitary, pluralist and radical.

The unitary, pluralist and radical views of organisation can be characterised in the terms shown in Table 1.1.

Table 1.1: Unitary, pluralist and radical frames of reference

	Unitary	Pluralist	Radical
Interests	Places emphasis on the achievement of common objectives. The organisation is viewed as being united under the umbrella of common goals and striving toward their achievement in the manner of a well-integrated team.	Places emphasis on the diversity of individual and group interests. The organisation is regarded as a loose coalition that has just a passing interest in the formal goals of the organisation.	Places emphasis on the oppositional nature of contradictory 'class' interests. Organisation is viewed as a battleground where rival forces (e.g. management and unions) strive for the achievement of largely incompatible ends.
Conflict	Regards conflict as a rare and transient phenomenon that can be removed through appropriate managerial action. Where it does arise it is usually attributed to the activities of deviants and troublemakers.	Regards conflict as an inherent and ineradicable characteristic of organisational affairs and stresses its potentially positive or functional aspects.	Regards organisational conflict as inevitable and as part of a wider class conflict that will eventually change the whole structure of society. It is recognised that conflict may be suppressed and thus often exists as a latent rather than a manifest characteristic of both organisations and society.
Power	Largely ignores the role of power in organisational life. Concepts such as authority, leadership and control tend to be preferred means of describing the managerial prerogative of guiding the organisation towards the achievement of common interests.	Regards power as a crucial variable. Power is the medium through which conflicts of interest are alleviated and resolved. The organisation is viewed as a plurality of power holders drawing their power from a plurality of sources.	Regards power as a key feature of organisation, but a phenomenon that is unequally distributed and follows class divisions. Power relations in organisations are viewed as reflections of power relations in society at large, and as closely linked to wider processes of social control, e.g. control of economic power, the legal system and education.

(Source: Based on Burrell and Morgan, 1979, pp. 204–388)

According to Morgan, a political take on organisations generally reflects a 'pluralist' frame of reference that emphasises competition between different interests and sources of power. This contrasts with a unitary view where the interests of the individual and the whole are synonymous, or the radical view 'class war' between deeply differentiated interests – a 'them' and 'us' approach. He suggests that some organisations can encompass all three approaches in different sections of the organisation.

 Stop and reflect

Which frame of reference applies to your organisation? Use the material in the table to work out the features that you observe.

Dealing with complexity

What all of this means is that the world of organisations is very complex, and it is difficult, if not impossible, to create a coherent picture at any one time of what is happening within and externally to the organisation. Karl

Weick, an American psychologist, sees organisations as sense-making systems that socially construct their realities by making sense of what is going on both within and outside the organisation (Weick, 1995). Members explore issues and hold conversations that allow them to create a 'reality' that they can understand. The following extract sets out some of Weick's key ideas.

Sensemaking is rolling hindsight. It is a continual weaving of sense from beliefs, from implicit assumptions, from tales from the past, from unspoken premises for decision and action, and from ideas about what will happen as a result of what can be done. Once put into words it is constrained and framed by those same words because they are only approximately what they refer to. Often words have multiple meanings, so all the time people are working with puns. Further, words are inclined to convey discrete categories: they are not equal to depicting the unbroken, complex flow of life in organizations.

The sense that is made is shaped also by selective perception, that is, by noticing some things and not others. Commitments that have been made then have to be justified retrospectively. There is a constant process of putting together reasoned arguments and arguing about them, most obviously in meetings which have a value as sensemaking occasions. However, the sense that is made has its limits. People with time to spend on a problem at a meeting make sense of it in a way most understandable to themselves, so others become less able to follow what is afoot. Showing up at meetings therefore produces a situation that is manageable only by those who have been showing up.

The whole sensemaking process gives ostensible orderliness to what is going on, and has gone on. The development of a 'generic sensemaking', within which individuals differ yet sufficiently concur, maintains a sense of organization …

Whatever the form of organization, it will have to work with ambiguous, uncertain, equivocal and changing information. Despite their facade of numbers and objectivity and accountability, organizations and those who manage them wade amidst guesswork, subjectivity and arbitrariness. Weick feels that language could better reflect this constant ambiguous flux by making more use of verbs and less of nouns. Indeed, he urges people to 'stamp out nouns': to think of managing rather than management, of organizing rather than organization …

He offers managers and others in organizations ten further 'pieces of advice':

1 Don't panic in the face of disorder. Some degree of disorder is necessary so that disorderly, ambiguous information can be taken in and coped with, rather than tidily screened out.

2 You never do one thing all at once. Whatever you do has many ramifications, not just the one you have in mind. And whilst some consequences happen right away, others show up indirectly and much later.

3 Chaotic action is preferable to orderly inaction. When someone asks 'What shall I do?' and is told 'I don't know, just do something', that is probably good advice. Since sense is made of events retrospectively, an action, any action, provides something to make sense of. Inaction is more senseless.

4 The most important decisions are often the least apparent. Decisions about what is to be retained in files, in databases, in memories indeed, provide the basis for future action. Such decisions may not be conspicuous, yet they sustain the past from which the future is begun.

5 There is no solution. As there are no simple answers, and rarely is anything right or wrong, learn to live with improvisation and just a tolerable level of reasonableness.

6 Stamp out utility. Good adaptation now rules out some options for the future. Concentrating overmuch on utility now can rule out sources of future utility. Resources and choices are used up. Better to retain some noise and variability in the system, even at a cost to present efficiency, so that fresh future repertoires of action may be opened up.

7 The map is the territory. When the managers' map of what causes what, drawn from past experience, is superimposed on the future, it becomes for them the territory that it maps. Simplification though it is, such a map has been worked over more than any other product has, and is as good a guide as can be had.

8 Rechart the organizational chart. Do not be boxed in by its conventional form. See things as they work out and people as they are to you. See the chart in the way that it functions. For example, in the box on the chart for chairman write 'hesitancy', in the box for general manager write 'assertiveness', and so on, in the way people come over to you.

9 Visualize organizations as evolutionary systems. See what is evolving, and what you can and should change. Likewise, recognize what is not, and you cannot.

10 Complicate yourself! Consider different causes, other solutions, new situations, more complex alternatives, and take pleasure in the process of doing so.

(Source: Pugh and Hickson, 2007, pp. 124–9)

This means that organisations are complex dynamic systems that are difficult to describe except via snapshots of their reality at particular moments in time. The organisation is in a continuous state of becoming (Zeitz, 1980).

To what extent do Weick's ideas assist you in understanding the reality of your organisational world?

1.2: Organisational culture

An understanding of **organisational culture** is indispensable for managers and organisations. Managers need to be sensitive to various cultural dispositions of members and customers, whether managing locally or abroad. Alvesson suggests that insights into and reflections on organisational culture:

> may be useful in [relation] … to getting people to do the 'right' things in terms of effectiveness, but also for promoting more autonomous standpoints in relationship to dominant ideologies, myths, fashions, etc. To encourage and facilitate the thinking through of various aspects of values, beliefs and assumptions in industry, occupations and organisations seem to me a worthwhile task.
>
> (Alvesson, 2002, p. 2)

Understanding an organisation means understanding its culture.

The culture or climate of an organisation is made up of traditions, habits, ways of organising and patterns of relationships at work. If you think of organisations such as a school, hotel, airport, a church or a variety of other work organisations, you will notice how the 'atmosphere' differs between them; the different ways in which things are done; differing levels of energy and individual freedom; and, of course, different kinds of people (Molander, 1986, p. 14). For Clegg et al. (2005, p. 265) the concept of culture in organisations encompasses the following questions:

- How are things done in particular organisations?
- What is acceptable behaviour?
- What norms are members expected to use to solve problems of external adaptation and internal integration, and which ones do they actually use?

The word 'culture', as a concept in organisation and management studies, has its main roots in social anthropology, where it was used to refer to a community's shared way of life. It embraces the symbols, myths, stories, and so on, that are the manifestations and transmitters of that culture. In this view a culture is very much homogenous – reflecting the extreme patterns that shape organisational realities. Anthropologists have stressed how beliefs and values influence attitudes and behaviour. Classic anthropological research studied rituals, symbols, myths and stories as the most obvious manifestations of beliefs and values of other societies in other parts of the world. The concept of culture in organisational behaviour has become widely accepted in contributing to the understanding of and in influencing behaviour in organisations. However, like many concepts, it has been widely contested, too, as you will see in this section. The study of culture proves to be more problematic when applied to complex things such as organisations, as it is not always easy to observe and understand culture, for it tends to permeate subtly most aspects of organisational life (Bloisi et al., 2006).

Here we focus mainly on 'organisational culture'. This is a simple term describing a very complex concept. A simple starting definition was offered by Deal and Kennedy (1982) as 'the way we do things around here' – which is at once appealing and straightforward. But would it, if posed as a question about your own or any other organisation, be an easy one to answer? For one thing, an organisation's culture has, for all its members except newcomers, a taken-for-granted quality that can make it hard to recognise, except by contrasting it with a different culture.

Different cultures exist in different countries, in different organisations or even within a single organisation. Managers increasingly work across different cultures – whether in multinational organisations, or where organisations have merged or are collaborating, or in interdisciplinary or interdepartmental teams. Over the last few decades in countries such as the UK, Germany, Spain and France there has been a significant influx of immigrants from all over the world, bringing with them imported values, beliefs and norms about what is important and their perspectives about how things should be done in organisational settings. In such cases it is crucial to understand the effects that cultures can have. Managers have to recognise and build on cultural particularities, adapting organisational products and policies to local cultures and managing employees in a manner appropriate to their culture (Gabriel, 1999, p. 168).

This understanding and managing of these cultural differences has over the years become a vital ingredient of organisational success. Working with people from different ethnic and cultural backgrounds is a challenge and a source of opportunity for managers and organisational cultures (Bloisi et al., 2006, p. 684). However, 'organisational culture' usually refers to the less tangible aspects of an organisation's way of doing things and, in particular, to the shared cognitive, interpersonal and value orientations of its members. If we are using the term in this sense – referring to a shared 'mental programming' – then it is reasonable to distinguish between structure and culture. However, these two aspects of organisations are bound to be closely related: cultures are expressed in behaviour and artefacts, and different sorts of procedures and arrangements tend to generate or require different attitudes and outlooks. All of this demonstrates that, even if the terms seem simple, the ideas (not to mention the realities) are complex and subtle.

The aims of this section are to explore what is meant by organisational culture and to establish the importance of understanding your cultural context. This section will help you to develop this understanding by using some established frameworks for classifying cultures and by exploring the strengths and weaknesses of different types of cultures. These types tend to be referred to as: dominant culture, sub-culture, strong culture and weak culture. The distinctions of culture might seem subtle, but they matter to managers because, for example, managers are often charged with delivery of 'culture change' (usually to improve performance). Concepts such as dominant culture, sub-culture and strong and weak cultures can help you to 'read' situations and also help reflective managers to understand what impact they might have. These concepts also sometimes point directly to the managerial action you may have to take in certain circumstances.

Before you proceed, it is probably worth breaking the concept down a little. Consider a list of definitions of culture found in the academic literature.

Definitions of organisational culture

1   'Culture is the set of important understandings (often unstated) that members of a community share in common' (Sathe, 1983, p. 6).

2   '[Culture is] a set of understandings or meanings shared by a group of people. The meanings are largely tacit among the members, are clearly relevant to a particular group, and are distinctive to the group' (Louis, 1985, p. 74).

3   'A standard definition of culture would include the system of values, symbols, and shared meanings of a group including the embodiment of these values, symbols, and meanings into material objects and ritualized practices. … The "stuff" of culture includes customs and traditions, historical accounts be they mythical or actual, tacit understandings, habits, norms and expectations, common meanings associated with fixed objects and established rites, shared assumptions, and intersubjective meanings' (Sergiovanni and Corbally, 1984, p. vii).

4   '[Culture is] the pattern of shared beliefs and values that give members of an institution meaning, and provide them with the rules for behavior in their organization' (Davis, 1984, p. 1).

5   'To analyze why members behave the way they do, we often look for the values that govern behaviour … But as the values are hard to observe directly, it is often necessary to infer them by interviewing key members of the organisation or to content analyze artefacts such as documents and charters. However, in identifying such values, we usually note that they represent accurately only the manifest or espoused values of a culture. That is, they focus on what people say is the reason for their behaviour, what they ideally would like those reasons to be, and what are often their rationalizations for their behaviour. Yet, the underlying reasons for their behaviour remain concealed or unconscious. To really understand a culture and to ascertain more completely the group's values and overt behaviour, it is imperative to delve into the underlying assumptions, which are typically unconscious but which actually determine how group members perceive, think, and feel' (Schein, 1992, p. 3).

6   'In a particular situation the set of meanings that evolves gives a group its own ethos, or distinctive character, which is expressed in patterns of belief (ideology), activity (norms and rituals), language and other symbolic forms through which organisation members both create and sustain their view of the world and image of themselves in the world. The development of a worldview with its shared understanding of group identity, purpose, and direction are

products of the unique history, personal interactions, and environmental circumstances of the group' (Smircich, 1983, p. 56).

7 'Culture does not necessarily imply a uniformity of values. Indeed quite different values may be displayed by people of the same culture. In such an instance, what is it that holds together the members of the organisation? I suggest that we look to the existence of a common frame of reference or a shared recognition. There may not be agreement about whether these issues should be relevant or about whether they are positively or negatively valued ... They may array themselves differently with respect to that issue, but whether positively or negatively, they are all oriented to it' (Feldman, 1991, p. 154).

8 'When organisations are examined from a cultural viewpoint, attention is drawn to aspects of organisational life that historically have often been ignored or understudied, such as the stories people tell to newcomers to explain "how things are done around here", the ways in which offices are arranged and personal items are or are not displayed, jokes people tell, the working atmosphere (hushed and luxurious or dirty and noisy), the relations among people (affectionate in some areas of an office and obviously angry and perhaps competitive in another place), and so on. Cultural observers also often attend to aspects of working life that other researchers study, such as the organisation's official policies, the amounts of money different employees earn, reporting relationships, and so on. A cultural observer is interested in the surfaces of these cultural manifestations because details can be informative, but he or she also seeks an in-depth understanding of the patterns of meanings that link these manifestations together, sometimes in harmony, sometimes in bitter conflicts between groups, and sometimes in webs of ambiguity, paradox, and contradiction' (Martin, 2002, p. 3).

These quotations reflect some of the ways that 'culture' has been used by academics and practitioners. The most common feature throughout the various definitions is 'the use of the word "shared" and the reference to culture as that which is distinctive or unique to a particular context' (Martin, 2002, p. 58). Still, not all academics and practitioners agree on this representation of culture as shared and unique, and this will become more evident as the concept is explored in this section. The critical element is for these collections of fundamental assumptions to be shared and accepted by organisational members.

Now consider the following extract from a fictional story by Daniel Orozco (1995) called 'Orientation'.

Extract from 'Orientation' by Daniel Orozco

Those are the offices and these are the cubicles. That's my cubicle there, and this is your cubicle. This is your phone. Never answer your phone. Let the Voicemail System answer it. This is your Voicemail System Manual. There are no personal phone calls allowed. We do, however, allow for emergencies. If you must make an emergency phone call, ask your supervisor first. If you can't find your supervisor, ask Phillip Spiers, who sits over there. He'll check with Clarissa Nicks, who sits over there. If you make an emergency phone call without asking, you may be let go.

These are your IN and OUT boxes. All the forms in your IN box must be logged in by the date shown in the upper left-hand corner, initialed by you in the upper right-hand corner, and distributed to the Processing Analyst whose name is numerically coded in the lower left-hand corner. The lower right-hand corner is left blank. Here's your Processing Analyst Numerical Code Index. And here's your Forms Processing Procedures Manual.

You must pace your work. What do I mean? I'm glad you asked that. We pace our work according to the eight-hour workday. If you have twelve hours of work in your IN box, for example, you must compress that work into the eight-hour day. If you have one hour of work in your IN box, you must expand that work to fill the eight-hour day. That was a good question. Feel free to ask questions. Ask too many questions, however, and you may be let go.

(Orozco, 1995, p. 1)

The definitions of culture above probably alerted you to some underpinnings of what culture is, even though they emphasise and focus on different things. Keeping those definitions in mind, what does Orozco's fictional story begin to reveal about the culture of this organisation? Through the orientation of a person entering a new job you learn about 'the way things are done round here' – the unwritten rules, beliefs, norms, rituals, myths and language. The new person learns about what is acceptable behaviour in the office. The newcomer must quickly learn the rules of the game in order to become an accepted member. Orozco's 'Orientation' illustrates how organisations develop patterns of cultural assumptions that get passed on to new members.

Stop and reflect

How does your organisation (or one that you know well) relate to its environment? How do you communicate? What do you expect of people and relationships within the organisation? What constitutes successful results?

Orozco's story conveys some of the shared and accepted assumptions in the office. A picture of how things are done in this organisation begins to emerge. But how can you recognise and characterise an organisation's culture? Cultural models can provide you with interesting insights of organisations and can be used to illuminate and organise the information and impressions about organisations, helping you to understand some of the many complexities of managing in organisations. One such model is the use of metaphors, as suggested by Morgan, which provides an alternative approach to the concept of organisational culture and is illustrated below.

Metaphors of organisational culture

One of the easiest ways to grasp and 'see' the nature of an organization's culture is to try to view it as if you are a visitor from a foreign land. As one tries to look at the organization with fresh eyes, one can see the intangible 'social glue' that holds everything together: how the language, norms, values, rituals, myths, stories and daily routines form part of a coherent 'reality' that lends shape to how and what people do as they go about their work.

In understanding this 'social glue' (which like all glue sometimes does not stick as well as it might, producing a fragmented or divided 'culture') other ways of thinking about culture may be appropriate.

For example, try thinking about the corporate culture as an iceberg. Recognize that what you see on the surface is based on a much deeper reality. Recognize that the visible elements of the culture may be sustained by all kinds of hidden values, beliefs, ideologies and assumptions – questioned and unquestioned, conscious and unconscious. As a manager, recognize that it may not be possible to change the surface without changing what lies below.

Or try thinking about the corporate culture as an onion. Recognize that it has different layers. Recognize that one can penetrate beneath the rituals, ceremonies and symbolic routines to discover inner layers of mythology, folklore, hopes and dreams that eventually lead to the innermost values and assumptions that lend meaning to the outward aspects of the culture. Recognize that to impact or change the culture in any significant way it is necessary to address and perhaps change the values that lie at the core.

Or try thinking about the corporate culture as an umbrella. Look for the overarching values and visions that unite, or are capable of uniting, the individuals and groups working under the umbrella. Recognize that one's ability to mobilize or change any organization may depend on finding the umbrella that can unite potentially divergent individuals, groups and subcultures in pursuit of a shared vision of reality.

(Source: Morgan, 1989, pp. 157–8)

Whether working from the ideas outlined above or your preferred metaphor, you can see the difficulty here in studying culture – but the benefits of getting to grips with culture are that it can play a powerful role in supporting missions and strategies. There are several threads running through the concept. One concerns integration – 'social glue', 'overarching values and visions that unite' people in an organisation to work together in coordinated ways. Another thread, exemplified by the 'iceberg', is more about the hidden nature of culture (see Figure 1.4). Like an iceberg, some values and assumptions are 'invisible' and can only be deduced from more tangible aspects or manifestations of culture.

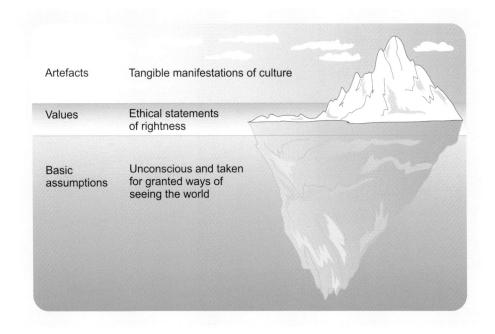

Figure 1.4: Schein's iceberg model of culture

Schein's iceberg model (1992) is useful in that it illustrates that there are visible cultural aspects of an organisation but that there are also elements of culture that are hidden and difficult to interpret. What is visible, for example, are things such as written documents – strategic plans, job descriptions and disciplinary procedures. But if organisational culture, as we have indicated so far, consists of values, beliefs and norms, Schein argues that these exist in people's heads, which raises the challenge of how actually to identify and interpret them. The key to Schein's idea is that these three levels of analysis can create a better understanding of the different components of culture in organisations.

Artefacts

These are the most tangible aspects that embody organisational culture, such as the type of people employed (personalities, levels of education, etc.), traditions and rituals, technology, architecture, logos, heroes, stories, myths, and so on. In the iceberg model, this is what is visible to everybody but which does not necessarily reveal everything about an organisation's culture. We can take architecture as an example here, how the rich and powerful often build the most impressive buildings as signs of success or artefacts of power – such as in the Canary Wharf business district in the City of London where successful investment banks have set up their headquarters and the Petronas Twin Towers, KLCC, Malaysia.

Stop and reflect

Can you think of other examples from around the world that illustrate this point?

The Petronas Twin Towers, KLCC, Malaysia

Values

These represent the invisible facets of organisational culture and include the norms and beliefs that employees express when discussing organisational issues, such as the value placed on (and rewards offered for) honesty, trust and effort. Values can also be represented in mission statements, such as Oxfam's, as shown above. You can see how these values can become visible or be brought to light through careful and directed questioning. And in the Oxfam example above, you are left in no doubt about what the organisational commitment is.

Oxfam
An international charity that works to alleviate poverty and injustice in countries around the world

Basic assumptions

These are almost impossible to see on the surface and are hidden beneath artefacts and expressed values – yet these are the most important. They include basic assumptions that shape members' world views, beliefs and norms, which guide behaviour but are not explicitly expressed, making it harder to observe them. This is also a challenge for managers because it is quite a challenge to change something that you cannot see, but what is certain is that basic assumptions profoundly influence a person's actions. Another issue to consider is that if some of these assumptions are taken for granted, how are they created? Do they change over time as personnel change? These questions might also explain why organisations try to select only people who will not challenge established beliefs when they are recruiting.

In Schein's examination of these issues, he goes on to provide a list of seven dimensions that he argued provided the basic cultural assumptions that construct different societies and organisations (see Table 1.2).

Table 1.2: Schein's dimensions of organisational culture

Dimension	Questions to be answered
1 The organisation's relation to its environment	Does the organisation perceive itself to be dominant, submissive, harmonising, searching out a niche?
2 The nature of human activity	Is the 'correct' way for humans to behave to be dominant/pro-active, harmonising, or passive/fatalistic?

3 The nature of reality/truth	How do we define what is true and what is not true, and how is truth ultimately determined both in the physical and social world? By pragmatic test, reliance on wisdom or social consensus?
4 The nature of time	What is our basic orientation in terms of past, present and future, and what kinds of time units are most relevant for the conduct of daily affairs?
5 The nature of human nature	Are human beings basically good, neutral or evil, and is human nature perfectible or fixed?
6 The nature of human relationships	What is the 'correct' way for people to relate to each other, to distribute power and affection? Is life competitive or cooperative? Is the best way to organise society on the basis of individualism or groupism? Is the best authority system autocratic/ paternalistic or collegial/participative?
7 Homogeneity versus diversity	Is the group better off if it is highly diverse or if it is highly homogeneous, and should individuals in a group be encouraged to innovate or conform?

Asking the same questions posed by Schein in relation to your own organisation or one that you know well could allow you to gain some insights into its overall culture. It should be noted, however, that this model has led to various disputes about the number and type of dimensions.

Culture as symbols

Another way to look at culture is through the symbols in which culture is manifest. Some symbols are obvious, some less so. The obvious or '*high-profile*' symbols are those designed to create an external image: the mission statement, the logo, the annual report, the corporate dress code, the head office architecture.

The '*low-profile*' symbols are those less tangible manifestations of what actually goes on inside an organisation in order to get work done. The two do not always match up. For example, at the height of its safety problems in early 2010, Toyota, the world's largest car manufacturer, was severely criticised: 'This system of quality control that Toyota represents to be at the heart of their corporation, doesn't reflect reality'; the source of the trouble was blamed on a 'Toyota culture which teaches that these are issues that should not be aired in public' with the company being 'at times more concerned with profit than with customer safety' (Foley, 2010). These comments point to a case where the low-profile symbols had became visible to the public and conflicted with the high-profile symbols to disastrous effect.

Low-profile symbols were studied by Trice and Beyer (1984), who suggest that they can be divided into four categories: practices, communications, physical forms and a common language.

- Practices – these are the rites, rituals and ceremonies of the organisation, and they take many forms – rituals for making tea or coffee; department or work group outings for meals or drinks; the annual office party; the doctor's 'rounds' in a hospital ward; the award night for 'salesperson of the year'; the visit of the director to a regional office; long-service award ceremonies, etc. Does your organisation or one that you know well carry out some of these practices?

- Communications – these are the stories, myths, sagas, legends, folk tales, symbols and slogans that are circulated in organisations. These stories are told and retold by members of the organisation and come to influence behaviour. These myths and legends illustrate the preferred way of performing and become goals to aim for.

- Physical forms – low-profile symbols of an organisation's culture manifest themselves in many physical ways. Examples include the appearance and location of the building; open plan or individual offices; posters or art work on walls; a single restaurant or an office canteen for most employees, with a separate dining room for managers; suits or casual attire; provision and distribution of flipcharts or whiteboards; the furniture (and again whether the type/luxuriousness of the furniture depends on a person's grade).

- A common language – jargon is common to many organisations. It is a convenient shorthand form of communication, but it also affects behaviour. McDonald's refers to its restaurant staff as 'crew members' and Disney employees are 'cast members'. These terms give added meaning to working at these places. The emphasis is on being part of a team – recruits may feel 'outsiders' until they have learned the language. However, this language is intended to affect the way the people respond to their work.

Here are some examples of organisational symbols.

The famous 'golden arches' logo at a McDonald's restaurant

Inside Google's China office

Arsenal Football Club's stadium in London, UK

From a consideration of Schein's levels of culture and the definitions, metaphors and symbols examined above, you should now be gaining a clearer idea of what tends to be encompassed by the idea of 'culture'.

Types of organisational culture

Over the last few decades there have been numerous attempts made by researchers to identify predominant types of organisational culture. The idea of culture, as the discussion thus far shows, is extremely complex, but this has not deterred writers from offering their perspectives. Looking at these models offers another way of understanding culture by distinguishing it according to recurring types. You must remember that all models are simplifications, and many of the more popular models of culture are extreme simplifications designed to be neatly placed within a particular type. Some focus on one or more dimensions of the idea of culture, others identify a small number of differing cultures and label and describe these. Two ways of categorising organisational cultures, and one approach to categorising national cultures, will be examined below. Before proceeding to these models, however, it is perhaps worth considering some of the perceived benefits of classifying cultures. For Gabriel:

> The first of these is that by being able to classify culture, a relationship or connection to other crucial organizational variables such as leadership style, structure and performance could be found which could be beneficial to you as a manager. Secondly, this might enable you to make a number of generalizations about the work experiences of those working in each type of culture, such as job satisfaction, career prospects or prevalent emotions.

> (Gabriel, 1999, p. 203)

Deal and Kennedy's model of organisational culture

Deal and Kennedy's model (1982), based on two dimensions, suggested that the biggest single influence on a company's culture was the business environment in which it operated. They called this 'corporate culture', which they asserted embodied what was required to succeed in that environment. The two key dimensions were the degree of **risk** associated with the company's activities, and the speed at which companies – and their employees – get **feedback** on whether decisions or strategies are successful. By 'feedback' Deal and Kennedy do not mean just bonuses, promotions and pats on the back. They use the term much more broadly to refer to knowledge of results. In this sense, a goalkeeper gets instant feedback from making a great save, but a surgeon may not know for several days whether an operation is successful, and it may take months or even years to discover whether a decision about a new product is correct. Deal and Kennedy distinguish between quick and slow feedback. Also, by splitting each dimension into high and low they came up with four 'generic' cultures, as shown in Figure 1.5.

Figure 1.5: Deal and Kennedy's model of organisational culture

The tough guy, macho culture

> A world of individualists who regularly take high risks and get quick
> feedback on whether their actions were right or wrong.
>
> (Deal and Kennedy, 1982, p. 107)

This type of culture is commonly thought to be prevalent in organisations in
which feedback comes in the form of financial rewards. You can think here
of commodity brokers and sales-orientated organisations, such as those that
sell water purifiers or financial services. Feedback, however, can come in
many other ways. Police officers, sports people and entertainers all receive
rapid feedback on the effectiveness of their work, and they could all be
classified as belonging to a 'tough guy' culture, even though their feedback
is not simply financial. Similarly, all these occupations have a degree of
inherent risk, and the line between success and failure can be very fine
indeed. For example, a football manager's career could rest on one
refereeing decision, and a comedian's success depends on the mixture of
people in the audience.

Managers in this type of culture need to be able to make decisions quickly
and to accept risk. To survive when things go wrong, they need to be
resilient. These cultures are characterised by aggressive internal competition.
Employees in such organisations believe that to get on they must be as tough
as the 'movers and shakers' at the top. These activities tend to produce a lot
of internal politics and conflict. In addition, these cultures tend to nurture
short-term views, and here you might recall some of the reasons that are
believed to have led to the fall of organisations such as Enron (auditing
failures in picking up billions in debt from failed deals and projects) and
Lehman Brothers Bank (bad debts led to its eventual collapse). Despite the
label 'tough guy', Deal and Kennedy suggest that this culture is the least

discriminatory of the four because it is, in their view, a meritocracy in which success is what is acknowledged and rewarded.

The work hard/play hard culture

> Fun and action are the rule here, and employees take few risks, all with quick feedback; to succeed, the culture encourages them to maintain a high level of relatively low-risk activity.
>
> (Deal and Kennedy, 1982, p. 108)

This type of culture is characterised by high levels of activity, and each employee has to take few risks. Instead, success is measured by persistence. Typically, the primary cultural value is to supply customers with a quality product or service. These cultures spawn meetings, conventions, team-working, office parties, jargon, buzzwords, and so on. They are typical of large organisations such as the motor industry, IT and telecoms because in smaller organisations there are often increased levels of risk as 'every decision is a big one'. The high levels of energy create two main problems for a manager: ensuring that the energy is being directed at the right tasks, and ensuring that quality accompanies the high levels of activity. For these reasons, IBM put up 'Think' signs all around the company.

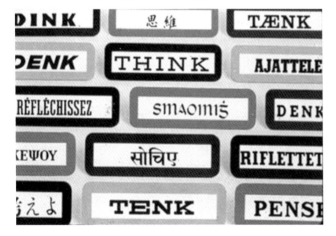

IBM 'Think' signs

The bet-your-company culture

> Cultures with big-stakes decisions, where years pass before employees know whether decisions have paid off. A high-risk, slow-feedback environment.
>
> (Deal and Kennedy, 1982, p. 108)

This type of culture is found in organisations involved in projects that consume large amounts of resources and take a long time to be realised. Examples include an aerospace organisation deciding to develop a new aircraft, such as Airbus, which has spent many years developing its new A380. Other examples would include a construction company building a skyscraper or an oil company that starts drilling in a new region. Each of these projects is very risky and the organisation does everything it can to ensure it makes the right decisions initially. Meetings become very important and experts are drawn in to give their opinions.

The process culture

> A world of little or no feedback where employees find it hard to measure what they do; instead they concentrate on how it's done. We have another name for this culture when the processes get out of control – bureaucracy!

> (Deal and Kennedy, 1982, p. 108)

Process cultures get a bad press from nearly all quarters. They are the bureaucracies, awash with red tape and memos. Their low-risk, slow-feedback environment means that employees become more concerned with how work is done – the process – than with what the work is. There is a danger that artificial environments develop, detached from the real world. Employees in these cultures may be very defensive. They fear and assume that they will be attacked when they have done things incorrectly. To protect themselves they engage in behaviour such as circulating emails copied to everyone remotely concerned with the issue.

Deal and Kennedy admit that this four-culture model is simplistic, but it can be a useful starting point for looking at your own organisation. A mix of all four cultures may be found within a single organisation. Furthermore, they suggest that companies with very strong cultures will skilfully blend the best elements of all four types in a way that allows them to remain responsive to a changing environment. Although these cultures have been criticised, for example, because customers fear the high-risk attitudes of those in a tough guy culture or the thoughtless energy of those in a work hard/play hard culture, they exist because they bring order to organisations and ensure that certain procedures are followed. Yet few organisations fall neatly into one of these four types, and it is very hard to relate these types to psychological personalities.

Stop and reflect

What sort of culture would you want in your organisation or, for example, looking after your life savings?

Think also about equity. Bureaucracy in public service undoubtedly makes services unresponsive, but it also ensures greater consistency, equity and impartiality of service – all of which rightly command high priority in public service organisations.

Handy's four types of organisational cultures

Another model of culture, popularised by Charles Handy (1999) – and following work by Harrison (1972) – also presents organisational cultures as classified into four major types: the power culture, the role culture, the task culture and the person or support culture. Handy's approach may help you understand why you have been more comfortable in some organisations than others. Interestingly, although Handy chooses to talk about *culture*, he shows the *structures* associated with his culture types. This may be because of the difficulty of drawing something as diffuse as culture, but it also reinforces the fact that culture and structure are interrelated.

Power culture

Handy illustrates the power culture as a spider's web (see Figure 1.6), with the all-important spider sitting in the centre 'because the key to the whole organisation sits in the centre, surrounded by ever-widening circles of intimates and influence. The closer you are to the spider, the more influence you have' (1999, p. 86). Organisations with this type of culture can respond quickly to events, but they are heavily dependent for their continued success on the abilities of the people at the centre; succession is a critical issue. They will tend to attract people who are power orientated and politically minded, who take risks and do not rate security highly. Control of resources is the main power base in this culture, with some elements of personal power at the centre.

Figure 1.6: Power culture

Size is a problem for power cultures. They find it difficult to link too many activities and retain control; they tend to succeed when they create new organisations with a lot of independence, although they usually retain central financial control.

This type of culture relies heavily on individuals rather than on committees. In organisations with this culture, performance is judged on results, and such organisations tend to be tolerant of means. They can appear tough and abrasive and their successes can be accompanied by low morale and high turnover as individuals fail or opt out of the competitive atmosphere. Working in such organisations requires that employees correctly anticipate what is expected of them from the powerholders and perform accordingly. If managers get this culture right, it can result in a happy, satisfied organisation that in turn can breed quite intense commitment to corporate goals. Anticipating wrongly can lead to intense dissatisfaction and sometimes lead to a high labour turnover as well as a general lack of effort and enthusiasm. In extreme cases, a power culture is a dictatorship, but it does not have to be.

Stop and reflect

What kind of manager do you think would be happy in a power culture?

Role culture

The role culture can be illustrated as a building supported by columns and beams: each column and beam has a specific role to play in keeping up the building; individuals are role occupants but the role continues even if the individual leaves. This culture shares a number of factors in common with Weber's (1952) description of the 'ideal-type' bureaucracy.

Figure 1.7: Role culture

This type of organisation is characterised by strong functional or specialised areas coordinated by a narrow band of senior management at the top and a high degree of formalisation and standardisation; the work of the functional areas and the interactions between them are controlled by rules and procedures defining the job, the authority that goes with it, the mode of communication and the settlement of disputes.

Position is the main power source in the role culture. People are selected to perform roles satisfactorily; personal power is frowned upon and expert power is tolerated only in its proper place. Rules and procedures are the chief methods of influence. The efficiency of this culture depends on the rationality of the allocation of work and responsibility rather than on individual personalities. This type of organisation is likely to be successful in a stable environment, where the market is steady, predictable or controllable, or where the product's life cycle is long, as used to be the case with many UK public sector bodies. Conversely, the role culture finds it difficult to adapt to change; it is usually slow to perceive the need for it and to respond appropriately. Such an organisation will be found where economies of scale are more important than flexibility or where technical expertise and depth of specialisation are more important than product innovation or service cost – for example, in many public service organisations.

For employees, the role culture offers security and the opportunity to acquire specialist expertise; performance up to a required standard is rewarded on the appropriate pay scale, and possibly by promotion within the functional area. However, this culture is frustrating for ambitious people who are power orientated, want control over their work or are more interested in results than method. Such people will be content in this culture only as senior managers. The importance of Handy's role culture is that it suggests that bureaucracy itself is not culture-free.

Stop and reflect

What kind of manager do you think would be happy in a role culture?

Task culture

Task culture is job- or project-oriented, and its accompanying structure can be best represented as a net (see Figure 1.8). Some of the strands of the net are thicker or stronger than others, and much of the power and influence is located at the interstices of the net, at the knots. Task cultures are often associated with organisations that adopt matrix or project-based structural designs.

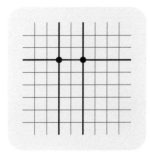

Figure 1.8: Task culture

The emphasis is on getting the job done, and the culture seeks to bring together the appropriate resources and the right people at the right level in order to assemble the relevant resources for the completion of a particular project. A task culture depends on the unifying power of the group to improve efficiency and to help the individual identify with the objectives of the organisation. So it is a team culture, where the outcome of the team's work takes precedence over individual objectives and most status and style differences. Influence is based more on expert power than on position or personal power, and influence is more widely dispersed than in other cultures.

Task culture depends on team work to produce results. Groups, project teams or task forces are formed for a specific purpose and can be re-formed, abandoned or continued. The organisation can respond rapidly since each group ideally contains all the decision-making powers required. One example of a task culture is NASA, the US space agency, which in the 1960s had the specific task of putting a man on the moon before the end of the decade and bringing him back safely. Individuals find that this culture offers a high degree of autonomy, judgement by results, easy working relationships within groups and mutual respect based on ability rather than on age or status.

The task culture is therefore appropriate when flexibility and sensitivity to the market or environment are important, where the market is competitive, where the life of a product is short and/or where the speed of reaction is critical. Against this must be set the difficulty of managing a large organisation as a flexible group, and of producing economies of scale or great depth of expertise.

Control in these organisations can be difficult. Essential control is retained by senior managers, who concentrate on the allocation of projects, people and resources, but they exert little day-to-day control over methods of working or procedures, without violating the norms of the culture. This works well in favourable circumstances and when resources are available for those who can justify using them. However, when resources are not freely available, senior managers begin to feel the need to control methods as well as results, and team leaders may begin to compete for resources, using political influence. Morale in the work groups tends to decline and the job becomes less satisfying in itself, so that employees begin to reveal their own objectives. This necessitates the introduction of rules and procedures, the use of position or the control of resources by managers to get the work done. So the task culture has a tendency to change to a role or power culture when resources are limited or when the whole organisation is unsuccessful.

Most managers, certainly at the middle and junior levels, prefer to work in the task culture, with its emphasis on groups, expert power, rewards for results and a merging of individual and group objectives. It is most in tune with the current trends of change and adaptation, individual freedom and low status differentials – but it may not be an appropriate culture for all circumstances.

Stop and reflect

What kind of manager do you think would be happy in a task culture?

Person culture

Person culture is an unusual culture. It is not found in many organisations, yet many people espouse some of its values. This type of culture is illustrated by a loose cluster or a constellation of stars (see Figure 1.9). In this culture the individual is the focal point; if there is a structure or an organisation, it exists only to serve and assist the individuals within it, to further their own interests without any overriding objective.

Clearly, not many organisations can exist with this sort of culture, or produce it, since organisations tend to have some form of corporate objective over and above the personal objectives of those who comprise them.

Figure 1.9: Person culture

Furthermore, control mechanisms, and even management hierarchies, are impossible in these cultures except by mutual consent. An individual can leave the organisation, but the organisation seldom has the power to evict an individual. Influence is shared and the power base, if needed, is usually expert; that is, people do what they are good at and are listened to for their expertise.

Consultants – both within organisations and freelance workers – and architects' partnerships often have this person-orientation. So do some universities. A cooperative may strive for the person culture in organisational form, but as it develops it often becomes, at best, a task culture, or often a power or role culture.

Although it would be rare to find an organisation in which the person culture predominated, you will often encounter people whose personal preferences are for this type of culture, but who find themselves operating in more orthodox organisations. Specialists in organisations, such as computer people in a business organisation, consultants in a hospital, architects in local government and university teachers benefit from the power of their professions. Such people are not easy to manage. Being specialists, alternative employment is often easy to obtain, and they may not acknowledge anyone as being in a position to exercise expert power greater than their own. Position power not backed up by resource power means nothing to such people, and coercive power is not usually available. They may not be influenced by group norms or relationships with colleagues, which might be expected to moderate their personal preferences. This leaves only personal power – and such people are often not easily impressed by personality.

 Stop and reflect

- What kind of manager do you think would be suited to a person culture?
- Which of Handy's categories is closest to your own organisation or department?
- Identify a successful colleague and consider how they got ahead.
- To what extent does this colleague display the attributes Handy suggests are best suited to the culture of your organisation?
- To what extent do you display those attributes? How useful do you find Handy's model?

There are limitations to Handy's approach. There is a tendency to take Handy's four cultures as fixed, or 'given', styles – something an organisation has, rather than something that is created, negotiated and shared by everyone involved in the organisation and which may evolve over time. None of the four types can claim to be better or superior; they are each suited to different types of circumstances. Most real-life organisations tend to involve a mixture of cultures, and in Handy's view each is suited to different types of circumstances, including different types of personalities.

Theories of types of culture offer caricatures and simplifications of complex phenomena; the real world is always richer and more subtle. One way of gaining an insight into these complexities has been to explore the link between national culture and organisational culture. Before you consider this approach, you may find it helpful to reflect upon the two models you have considered so far.

Stop and reflect

- How does Deal and Kennedy's model compare with Handy's?
- What do their different approaches have in common?
- Within which cultures, identified by the different authors, would you prefer to be a manager – and to be managed?

National cultures and organisational culture

In this sub-section you will explore the nation as a 'source' of culture. 'You are undoubtedly aware of the cultural differences among countries, whether you have travelled outside your home country or simply read and watched TV and movies. For instance Arab cultures differ from Asian, Mediterranean, African and western European cultures' (Bloisi et al. 2006, p. 685). The idea that a nation has a particular set of beliefs and values, a shared set of practices or a way of behaving has alerted practitioners to the need to understand other cultures in order to conduct business effectively (Holden, 2002). It has been argued that when organisations move into foreign countries or when many of their new employee recruits are from other countries, this has created many challenges for management practices, as some of the common values that might be shared begin to differ across national cultures (such as 'providing excellent services to customers') (Halsall, 2008). This section therefore highlights the ways in which national cultural differences affect and are reflected in organisations, as well as drawing your attention to some of the bases on which sub-cultures can emerge within organisations.

In order to gain an understanding of national culture and its interaction with organisational culture, summaries of the seminal research on this subject of Hofstede (1994, 2001) and Trompenaars and Hampden-Turner (2003) are offered below. Others working in this field (e.g. Jacob, 2005) believe that national cultures are too complex to be explained in terms of following a consistent path of progression dimensions, as used by Hofstede and Trompenaars. As a possible solution, Rarick and Nickerson (2008, p. 9) propose 'that a better understanding of national culture can be developed through a combination of approaches in which weaknesses of one model can be supplemented by the qualities of another'.

The Hofstede framework

Hofstede's cultural difference model has typically formed the basis for identifying differences in national cultures in university management courses. His research looking at well over 100,000 IBM employees in 53 subsidiaries covering 50 countries provides an insightful look at the similarities and differences in cultural values. The essence of national culture for Hofstede is what he terms 'national mental programming', which is that part of our collective learning 'that we share with other members of our nation, region, or group but not with members of other nations, regions, or groups' (Hofstede, 1983, p. 76). He suggests that four dimensions discriminate between national cultures in the workplace.

Hofstede's four dimensions

Power distance – this is the extent to which a society expects a high degree of power difference between levels in an organisation. A high score reflects a belief in an established hierarchy, while a low score reflects a belief in equal rights.

Uncertainty avoidance – this is the extent to which society willingly accepts ambiguity and risk. High score societies are risk averse.

Individualism (as opposed to collectivism) – societies high on this emphasise the role of the individual and expect people to take care of themselves and their immediate family. Low score societies are more concerned with the greater good of the group.

Masculinity – a high score here reflects a society that holds values that in the West were traditionally male – competitiveness, assertiveness, ambition and concern for material possessions. A low score society would reflect a more nurturing orientation, emphasising consideration of others.

When Hofstede looked at how societies scored on these dimensions he found four major clusters within Europe:

1 A Germanic group (Germany, Austria, Switzerland) tending towards high masculinity and low power distance.

2 A mainly Scandinavian group (Sweden, Finland, Norway, Denmark but also the Netherlands) tending towards high individualism, low masculinity and low power distance.

3 An Anglo-Saxon group (Britain and Ireland) with high individualism and masculinity and low power distance and uncertainty avoidance.

4 A mainly Latin group (France, Spain, Italy, Portugal, Greece, but also Belgium) with high uncertainty avoidance and high power distance.

By comparison outside Europe, Japan scored highly on masculinity and uncertainty avoidance, while the USA scored highly on individualism but low on uncertainty avoidance.

Hofstede later added a fifth dimension 'Long term orientation' when Chinese researchers found differences between time orientations that differentiated between long-term orientations (e.g., 'perseverance' and 'thrift') and short-term orientations (e.g., 'respect for tradition' and 'protecting one's face') (Hofstede and Bond, 1988; Franke et al., 1991).

While this is again a highly simplified approach to a complex issue, you may find it a useful starting point for thinking about your experience of working with colleagues from different national backgrounds. Hofstede's work has, however, attracted a number of critics. For instance, McSweeney

(2002) and Smith (2002) have expressed concern about the generalisability of the samples, the levels of analysis, the comparison of political boundaries (countries) to culture and the validity of the instruments of measurement. The links between the dimensions as measured and actual behaviour to be found in organisations are also not made explicit. Hofstede's assumptions of the homogeneity of each studied culture have also been challenged by Sivakumar and Nakata (2001). Hofstede's use of masculinity/femininity as the label for his fourth dimension was unfortunate as this is an outdated way of describing what are really just two distinct approaches to interpersonal relationships at work. However, Hofstede's model, despite the criticism, has represented the most popular approach to cultural assessment (Rarick and Nickerson, 2008).

Stop and reflect

From your own experience, to what extent do you agree with Hofstede's descriptions?

The Trompenaars and Hampden-Turner framework

This framework built on the work of Hofstede by broadening the definition of national cultures in recognising that wider historical, political and social factors in a country may affect 'business values'. Their model is therefore a useful tool for understanding and dealing with cultural differences. Trompenaars and Hampden-Turner suggest that national cultures vary in how their members solve problems by identifying three major types:

1 The relationships with people – five major cultural differences were identified (see below).

2 Attitudes toward time – suggests that societies view time differently, as well as how the past, present and future interrelate.

3 Attitude towards the environment – relates to whether individuals are considered either a part of nature or separate from it; also how much individuals are a master of their fate.

The Trompenaars and Hampden-Turner framework further identify five major cultural differences in how relationships with other people are handled, and these are expressed as pairs of binary opposites (see Table 1.3).

Table 1.3: Trompenaars and Hampden-Turner cultural dimensions

1 Universalism versus the particular	A culture's application of principles. Universal: emphasis is on rules and regulations regardless of individual circumstances. Particular: emphasis on relationships and flexibility.
2 Individual versus collective	A culture's focus on either the group or the individual. An individual focus is on the needs of the individual, freedom and responsibility. A collective focus relates to group emphasis and consensus.
3 Neutral versus affective	Neutral: emphasises objectivity and detachment. Affective: emphasises displays of emotion.

4 Specific versus diffuse	A culture's blending of work and personal life. Specific: emphasises separation of the two. Diffuse: blends them.
5 Achievement versus prescription	A culture's way of assigning status. Achievement: emphasises performance. Prescription: emphasises that status comes from age, education, gender and personal characteristics.

This framework is useful in helping you link the dimensions of culture to other aspects of organisational behaviour. Two very important points that this framework brings up are, first, that increasingly, operating in a global environment where people and goods move to and fro one needs to be aware of cultural differences in order to avoid potential problems. Second, this framework also suggests that there is no single formula for reconciling cultural differences and it encourages viewing each culture on its own merit with no culture superior to another.

Whatever your experience of different cultural contexts, even the simple models considered in this section should have made you aware of the extent of cultural variation around you. Cultures can vary at the level of the individual work group, the department or the organisation. Overlaying this will be the influence of national cultures, whether because an organisation is operating multinationally or because it draws on a multicultural workforce.

Distinguishing corporate and organisational culture

The term 'culture' has been used in two different ways in reference to organisations. Smircich (1983) put the issue neatly when she asked whether culture is something an organisation *is* or something an organisation *has*. This points up the different ways in which the notion of culture can be viewed by theorists and practitioners.

If culture is something an organisation *has*, it can be treated as another variable to be manipulated or another contingency that affects structures and processes. As such, it could be seen to be 'owned' by management who disseminate it downwards throughout the organisation. With this perspective, culture can therefore be changed to improve efficiency or effectiveness in what has been referred to as 'cultural engineering' (Jackson and Carter, 2000, pp. 27–8) – creating the 'right' kind of organisational culture such that management-imposed values rule out particular courses of action or narrow the range of options for a decision. So what might cultural engineering look like in practice? You will look at a case study shortly – Nokia Siemens Networks at the beginning of tackling this process.

However, if culture is something an organisation *is*, it describes the negotiated and shared meanings that emerge from social interactions. Culture in this sense is created and re-created by its participants in a continuous process, which senior managers are part of and can influence but which they cannot determine or control. Clearly, used in this sense, those aspects of an organisation's culture that senior managers can shape and control are less than the whole of the culture. The distinction between the approaches to culture by management and practitioners was captured by Linstead and Grafton-Small (1992) who in their research contrasted 'corporate culture' and 'organisational culture'. They suggested that corporate culture was 'devised by management and transmitted, marketed, sold or imposed on the rest of the organisation … the rites, rituals, stories and values which are offered to organisational members … gaining their commitment' (p. 333). In contrast, 'organisational culture', they asserted 'grows or emerges within the organisation and emphasises the creativity of organisational members as culture makers', which appears to be a lot more realistic as it seems to acknowledge the presence of sub-cultures within the organisation.

The shaping and controlling of culture has attracted management and practitioners who have believed that strong cultures could be created to produce commitment, dedication, enthusiasm and even passion in workers. These ideas were put forward by Deal and Kennedy (1982), Peters and Waterman (1982) and Kanter (1984) who argued that a strong culture was crucial in organisational success as it enabled employees to be certain about what they thought and felt, making them more dedicated to the organisation. However, this view of culture has attracted a lot of criticism, too. Robbins (2001) has suggested that this emphasis on a strong culture contributed to the demise of some of the biggest corporations (for example, Barings Bank, Enron, WorldCom, Lehman Brothers). Willmott (2002) has also criticised strong cultures as privileging the views of managers of the organisation as a means of subordinating and incorporating other members, thus enforcing a uniformity of culture within the organisation.

You will consider this in more detail when you explore the subject of motivation.

So how might proponents of a strong culture reply to these objections? If they are wise, they will welcome them as clarifying the nature and scope of the culture-building that is being proposed. To this end it is helpful to distinguish between broad and narrow versions of culture, between culture in an all-encompassing sense and those aspects of an organisation's culture that senior managers can more or less control.

Having examined the arguments about strong culture, we now move on to look more closely at what is involved in promoting a corporate culture in which diverse perspectives on organisational problems and issues can be productively harnessed in organisational processes.

Managing cultural differences

Creating culture

Nokia Siemens Networks' birth involved more than merging product lines and operations. Soft issues rather than hard ones can kill a merger in its infancy, and considering the might and history of NSNs' parents, unifying two distinct corporate cultures into one would prove to be one of the venture's biggest challenges

In November 2006, 250 executives from Nokia Networks and Siemens Communications got together in a room in Munich, tasked with hashing out the details of their impending merger. Nokia and Siemens already had a good idea of what the company would look like on paper: They would create a huge global company with strengths in both wireless and wireline telecommunications, leverage a massive international sales force and achieve economies of scale unavailable to either company so long as they remained network divisions of their parent companies. But NSN also would be the merger of two distinct corporate cultures. Bastions of engineering in their own countries, Germany and Finland, each had their own deeply ingrained identities and, yes, pride. The numbers aside, how would the new NSN function?

Attending that meeting was Bosco Novak, who would become the head of human resources for the new joint venture. The president of Nokia Networks and future CEO of NSN, Simon Beresford-Wylie, had asked Novak to take over the role in July, two days before the merger agreement was publicly announced. At the time, Novak headed Nokia's global services division and supervised a huge multinational organization – and also had an inherent cultural asset: He was a German who had worked for Nokia since 2000. But Novak had not a lick of HR experience and was puzzled by his boss's choice. But Beresford-Wylie explained that his role wouldn't be that of an ordinary HR manager. Novak would be responsible for crafting and implementing an entirely new culture at NSN. Novak accepted and five months later he and 249 other executives, managers and engineers were trying to figure out what exactly that new NSN culture would be.

The group managed to find several fundamentals that the two companies had in common: They both were Western European; they both had an ingrained engineering culture; and their employees also had a deep pride in being on technology's cutting edge and a feeling of making a difference in the world. But those cram sessions also revealed some profound differences, not just in their surface organizations but in how their employees related to one another and management and in their approach to problems. Most striking of those differences was a sense of formality and structure in Siemens' culture, as opposed to a looser set of relationships and emphasis on flexibility at Nokia.

(Source: Fitchard, 2009)

The NSN case illustrates how senior managers begin to promote the adoption of a new corporate culture. Managing the differences that arise, whatever their origins, can present considerable challenges for a manager. You can see that managers from these two organisations coming together from different cultures may perceive requirements for meeting their commitment to customer service, for example, in different ways. These influences can and do lead to differences in preferred methods of pursuing goals, as illustrated by NSN. National cultural influences may colour perceptions of what is important as well, as informed by the works of Hofstede and Trompenaars and Hampden-Turner.

The NSN case illustrates the distinction between organisational and corporate culture and shows how proponents of a strong culture argue for promoting a homogeneous and consistent corporate culture (which is realistic and important) rather than a homogeneous and consistent organisational culture (which they accept is unrealistic and unnecessary). So, for example, a company such as NSN can and should share a distinctive corporate culture across Europe, even though its managers will represent many different culture areas and have different functional backgrounds. Managers and staff can behave and respond similarly in some respects, yet differ (perhaps considerably) in many other respects.

Many organisations, whether multinational or not, try to promote strongly shared guiding values such as customer service. Multinationals seek to embed such values to ensure that managers and workforce, irrespective of their diverse cultural backgrounds, pull in the same direction as they strive to achieve the same broad corporate aims and goals. Novak's task at NSN would be to arrive at new shared values and describe how these values are going to operate in the company. At the organisational level, the intention is not to suppress diversity of opinion about how best to achieve these aims and goals. It is stated that NSN has two very distinct differences, which imply a 'culture clash' and a challenge about whose culture will be adopted – which also has the potential to alienate the other group.

Stop and reflect

An organisation's culture, once established, rarely fades away – so how would Novak at NSN create a new organisational culture? Do differences between the cultures at NSN generate problems? What might reinforce and sustain this new culture once in place? How do new employees learn their organisation's culture?

The models that you have looked at thus far are useful tools for cultural analysis. Cultures may involve conflict as well as agreement, and divide just as much as they integrate. The new corporate values that managers attempt to promote through such methods may or may not become embedded in the organisation's culture in time. However, by creating behavioural expectations that accord with these values, managers help to generate the parameters within which initiative is exercised by those at lower organisational levels. They can perpetuate exclusions and inequalities just as much as a sense of belonging and identity. Attempts to force one culture on a group with very different values are fairly common, but may be counter-productive. A better understanding of why cultures differ, and of the value of such differences, may make such initiatives less likely, and remove much of the friction associated with working across cultural boundaries.

Stop and reflect

What problems have you observed or associated with working with different national or organisational cultures in your organisation or one that you know well? How have these been handled? Were there any tensions between dominant and subordinate cultures? What is your role in this?

Conclusion to Chapter 1

The first section of this chapter on organisations identified some of the factors that shape organisations. It was not exhaustive: there are many other theories that could have been examined. What the section tried to do was to move from commonplace ideas about what organisations are and why they exist to uncovering the ways that our thinking about organisations is shaped by the ideas and metaphors that we have in our heads. When you think that your job is complicated, we hope by now you realise that this is because managing and working in organisations is, indeed, a highly complex endeavour.

The second section of this chapter examined organisational culture. One of the well-developed views of organisational culture is that it is possible to create a culture that other members can be persuaded to accept, and that this coming together towards one shared common goal can lead to organisational success. This perspective accepts that some organisational values will be shaped by managers. However, this section has shown that, while it is plausible that managers can succeed in this to some extent, not all cultural inputs are likely to be completely adopted in the form intended by managers.

Other views have perceived this perspective as the source of the problem by enabling management to be dominant over subordinates and thus disempowering them. The different readings of culture have offered different perspectives, which bring insights into understanding organisational successes and failures. This critical stance on organisational culture asks you to acknowledge the other stakeholders in the organisation, who are not passive receivers of what management feeds them. There are many factors that have to be considered, all of which interrelate within an organisational culture. You also have to consider how national cultural differences affect organisational culture.

The challenges are many, as exposed in this chapter, but as a manager one of the fundamental questions for you is whether culture is available to be 'manipulated' by managers. Hopefully this chapter has shown you that you should be aware of culture and its consequences rather than assuming that you have the power to create and manage it.

2: Working with people
Introduction

In this chapter you are going to study the concept of motivation first, followed by the study of teams and groups. Understanding motivation is an important facet of managing and is crucial for organisations, as it is through people that organisations achieve or realise their goals. The theories that you will explore in this chapter should not be taken as if they were 'true' but should be read as a set of sophisticated and problematic ideas exploring the nature of human motivation. In the section on teams and groups you will consider why this has become an important area of interest for organisations and managers. This way of working and dividing work to accomplish tasks is accompanied by numerous challenges, while also offering much promise for the organisation and managers. By working through what happens first at an individual level and then to the group and organisation as the fundamental units of analysis, this section will help explain what happens to groups within organisations.

2.1: Motivation

Understanding what motivates people is a key management challenge. Individuals have a variety of changing – and often conflicting – needs and expectations, which they attempt to satisfy in a number of different ways. Thus, at any given time the motivation of individuals within the same workplace may vary considerably.

So what motivates people to work? Throughout most of the twentieth century, organisational practitioners, managers and researchers have sought to understand people's motivations. As summarised by Roberts (2007, p. 43), six key questions have been asked about motivation (the list probably includes some of the challenges you face in managing others). The questions are:

- What motivates a person? Should you look for the answer 'inside' the person in their 'needs' for money, status or power? Should you look outside at the work they do and how they are managed?
- Is there a universal truth to be discovered, or is motivation highly contingent and dependent on the specific character of a person or situation?
- How does motivation change over time? Is what motivates the same as what demotivates?
- Can your manager know more about what motivates you than you do, or does your motivation depend on the sense you make of your experiences?
- Can a manager motivate someone else or is motivation always something you get from yourself?
- What allows or gets in the way of such self-motivation?

What has emerged from these questions is that motivation is primarily about 'people's behaviour and feelings, and about their informal rather than formal organising' (Crowther and Green, 2004, p. 35), and as such, it is obviously an important aspect of managing. Part of your managerial role will therefore be to arrange conditions of work so that the members of your team are motivated to work (1) with maximum commitment and (2) in a way that meets organisational objectives.

As a manager, then, you will need to develop your understanding of this complex concept of motivation. One way to begin to do this is to look critically at established theories of motivation. In so doing you can become more aware of your own assumptions and perhaps change them in the process. As a result, you may begin to see new possibilities for the organisation of your own work and that of people who work with you. And this should in turn make work more rewarding and improve organisational performance.

Drawing on a rich variety of research into motivation, this section addresses the following questions:

1   What is motivation?

2   Why is motivation important at work?

3   What motivates individuals?

4   How do organisations motivate staff?

What is motivation?

There are a number of competing definitions of motivation. According to Dawson motivation refers to the 'mainspring of behaviour; it explains why individuals choose to expend a degree of effort towards achieving particular goals' (1986, p. 7), while for Rollinson motivation is:

> a state arising in the processes that are internal and external to the individual, in which the person perceives that it is appropriate to pursue a certain course of action (or actions) directed at achieving a specified outcome (or outcomes) and in which the person chooses to pursue those outcomes with a degree of vigour and persistence.
>
> (Rollinson, 2008, p. 148)

Another writer on motivation, Mullins (2008), defines motivation as a 'driving force' through which people strive to achieve their goals and fulfil a need or uphold a value.

Finally, according to Bloisi et al. (2006), there are three elements that are contained in definitions of motivation. These are:

1   some need, motive or goal that triggers action

2   a process that directs the choice of action

3   a level of effort intensity that is applied to the chosen vocation.

So, to summarise, needs, values and goals form the building blocks of motivation and can be defined as follows:

- Needs are fundamental requirements for survival and wellbeing, and can be physical or psychological.
- Values are things that people consider good or desirable, and culture plays an important role in deciding which ones become important. They are not usually specific to a particular situation.
- Goals are things that are sought in a particular situation in which culture also plays a significant role.

Thus, for example, you have a physiological need for food and, because money can buy that food, money will have a value. Your goal then might be to receive payment, and this goal might generate the action of seeking work. The key here is that when you do not have food or money, you are 'pushed' to go out searching for them (of course, not meeting these needs can have consequences, for example, starvation, illness or death). It is worth keeping these elements (i.e., needs, values, goals) clear, as some of the popular theories in the area of motivation emphasise different elements.

Stop and reflect

Think of your own experiences for a moment and reflect on your sources of motivation. What motivates you at the moment? Is it possible to explain this simply?

Next we will look at the two main groups of theories that focus on motivation. These are **content theories** and **process theories**.

Content theories focus on human needs and their satisfaction ('content' in this context refers to those '*contents*' within us that drive or push us: see Kornberger et al., 2008), whereas process theories were introduced because it was felt that content theories did not sufficiently explain why people are motivated to behave in certain ways and because to answer such questions it is necessary to consider what *processes* are involved in motivation.

Stop and reflect

Before we venture too far into detailed explanations of needs and other sources of motivation, take a few minutes to consider the following questions. It will get you thinking about personal applications of the motivational theories you are being introduced to in this section.

- How do you make it possible for members of your team, or people you want to work with, to gain desired goals repeatedly – so as to maintain their good job performance?
- What could your manager do to increase your motivation and commitment to work?

Keep these questions in mind as you read through the rest of this section. While you are reading about each of the models of motivation, think about how the models can help you answer these questions.

Content theories of motivation

When managers talk about theories of motivation, they often refer to Abraham Maslow and his hierarchy of needs theory. This is one of the most famous content theories of motivation.

Maslow's hierarchy of needs

Maslow's hierarchy of needs theory suggests that there are five categories of needs, organised from the most basic physiological needs to the highest-order **self-actualisation** needs (see Figure 2.1).

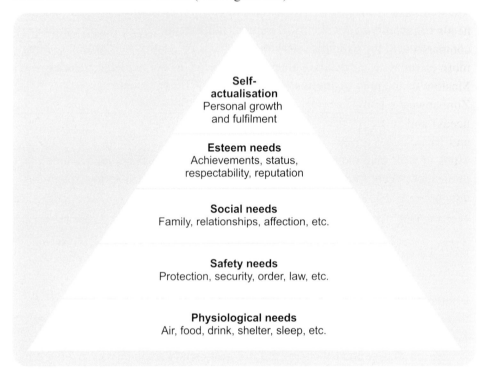

Figure 2.1: Maslow's hierarchy of needs (Source: adapted from Maslow, 1970)

According to Maslow, needs form a hierarchy, and people must satisfy their lower-level needs first. Thus, hungry, cold individuals will focus on getting food and warmth with no concern for their higher-order needs; but when well-fed and warm, they will seek safety and then the comfort of being with others. This means that people attend to higher needs only when they have satisfied the lower needs.

It is worth thinking about what can happen when needs are not satisfied, or when the source of satisfaction is removed or threatened. Try, for example, taking a bone away from a hungry dog – you will get a violent reaction. By analogy, if people perceive that some element that satisfies their current needs is likely to be removed, they, too, are likely to react adversely. An overtime ban, the threat of redundancy, a drop in the standard of working conditions can all produce adverse reactions, including drops in productivity, stress-related illnesses or industrial action.

However, the needs hierarchy is a generalisation. It may not help much with the value each individual places upon a particular reward or with changes in needs over time. The case of a hunger striker, for example, is difficult to explain by means of the needs hierarchy. However, Maslow has made an important contribution to our understanding of the behaviour of individuals by drawing attention to the importance of multiple motives. The needs hierarchy also gives us some indication of the needs people are seeking to fulfil and the rewards they hope to obtain from the workplace. In this respect, Maslow's theory is a useful starting point in assessing ways in which to motivate particular individuals in the workplace.

Because of its simplicity, Maslow's hierarchy of needs has an intuitive appeal among managers and practitioners. However, the theory has also attracted criticism for assuming that motivation is hierarchical, while research has failed to find support for a clear delineation of five sets of needs organised into a hierarchy. For instance, Harvey et al. (2000) in their comparative study come to different conclusions about the work values and motives of managers from Britain and Zimbabwe. Their findings suggest that Maslow's hierarchy might need to be re-ordered and redefined for Zimbabweans and others who put higher importance on security (safety needs) and self-esteem needs and less on accomplishment (self-actualisation) and friendship. In addition, people may have different priorities at different times in their life or at different stages of their career. They may also have all levels of need simultaneously (even someone close to self-actualisation will be upset if their salary is reduced). These are motivational issues that, as a manager, you need to become skilful at diagnosing.

Although Maslow originally theorised these issues over half a century ago (in 1943), elements of his theory still dominate management thinking today. For example, Kornberger et al. (2008, p. 251) draw on Maslow's insights in asserting that 'If people have to worry about where their next meal will come from, or where to sleep, or whether they have family support, how can they realize their potential?'

In addition to Maslow there are a number of other ways of categorising needs. Alderfer (1972), for example, contributed what has become known as ERG theory, which hypothesises that rather than five needs, individuals have in fact three needs. These needs are *existence* needs, *relatedness* needs and *growth* needs (thus, ERG).

1 Existence needs are concerned with sustaining human existence and survival. They cover the physiological and safety needs of a material nature.

2 Relatedness needs concern relationships with the social environment such as love or belonging, affiliation and meaningful interpersonal relationships of a safety or esteem nature.

3 Growth needs are concerned with the development of potential and cover self-esteem and self-actualisation.

The main similarities between Alderfer's and Maslow's theories are that (1) both hypothesise human needs as the basis for motivation, (2) both hypothesise similar types of needs (although the precise classifications differ) and (3) both theories view needs as being hierarchical. However, Alderfer suggests that extra rewards at the lower levels can compensate for a lack of satisfaction at the higher levels, whereas for Maslow a lower-level need must be satisfied first before proceeding to the next level.

More recently, Lawrence and Nohria (2002) have suggested that there are four main drives: to acquire, to bond, to learn and to defend. Lawrence and Nohria make the point that these four drives are 'hardwired', the result of aeons of evolution. In fact, evolution theory could be seen to support Maslow's hierarchy, too. Thus, if you believe in the survival of the fittest, an animal that does not concern itself with personal survival through immediate physiological need satisfaction and attention to personal safety will not leave many offspring. These needs being satisfied, in a social species at least, social needs then become important. Status will next contribute to breeding success, and self-actualisation and learning might help the social group as a whole. From this perspective, while the means of satisfying needs may be learned, at least some of the underlying drives may well be extremely deep-rooted and exert a strong influence on behaviour.

Hardwired
Pertaining to or being an intrinsic and relatively unmodifiable pattern of behaviour

Lawrence and Nohria also make the interesting suggestion that drives energise and partially steer not just behaviour but also reasoning, decision making, perception and memory.

Stop and reflect

- Which of the needs in Maslow's hierarchy are currently satisfied by your present job?
- Which of the needs in Alderfer's ERG theory are currently being satisfied by your present job?
- You may like to test out Lawrence and Nohria's theory of drives on your own experience:
  - Do you notice restaurants more when you are hungry?
  - Do you reason one way about food when you start a diet and then reason differently as you become seriously hungry?

The needs-based theories discussed so far illustrate the complexity of human behaviour. Needs vary within an individual over time, vary across people within an organisation or culture and vary across national cultures.

The next section will first turn the spotlight on managers through the work of McGregor, who suggests that behaviour at work is dependent on managers' assumptions. The section will then turn to look at Herzberg, who focuses on employees' needs and how work can be designed to motivate employees.

McGregor's Theory X/Theory Y

McGregor, in his studies of how managers manage and how they go about motivating others, reasoned that a manager's perspectives about people influence how they attempt to manage (McGregor, 1960). McGregor identifies two different sets of managerial assumptions about people, which he called **Theory X** and **Theory Y**. According to McGregor, in what became a critique of traditional management practices at the time, Theory X management is based on the following assumptions about people.

1   Management is responsible for organizing the elements of
    productive enterprise – money, materials, equipment, people – in
    the interest of economic ends.

2   With respect to people, this is a process of directing their efforts,
    motivating them, controlling their actions, modifying their behavior
    to fit the needs of the organization.

3   Without this active intervention by management, people would be
    passive – even resistant – to organizational needs. They must
    therefore be persuaded, rewarded, punished, controlled – their
    activities must be directed. ...

(Source: McGregor, 1989, p. 315)

McGregor suggests that Theory X helps us understand the assumptions
underlying a certain type of managerial approach. These Theory X
assumptions are, however, limiting for managers in that they can prevent
managers from seeing the potential benefits of other approaches and can
actually be the cause of employees becoming demotivated.

McGregor then put forward an alternative theory, *Theory Y*, which he argued
was based on more accurate assumptions about human nature and
motivation. McGregor claimed that:

1   Management is responsible for organizing the elements of
    productive enterprise – money, materials, equipment, people – in
    the interest of economic ends.

2   People are not by nature passive or resistant to organizational
    needs – they become so as a result of their experience in
    organizations.

3   The motivation, the potential for development, the capacity for
    assuming responsibility, the readiness to direct behavior towards
    organizational goals are all present in people. Management does
    not put them there. It is the responsibility of management to make
    it possible for people to recognize and develop these human
    characteristics for themselves.

4   The essential task of management is to arrange organizational
    conditions and methods of operation so that people can achieve
    their own goals best by directing their own efforts toward
    organizational objectives.

(Source: McGregor, 1989, p. 321)

Theory Y challenged accepted management practices. McGregor saw Theory
Y management as a way of aligning the goals of the employees with those
of the organisation. He suggested that if people can satisfy their personal

goals by accomplishing organisational objectives then this creates a win–win situation for both management and employees.

McGregor's Theory X and Theory Y can be seen as representing two extreme ends of a continuum of beliefs about management. At one end, Theory Y states that if you delegate authority and provide people with resources to do a job, you will find that people behave responsibly. However, if you manage according to Theory X, you might satisfy immediate lower-level organisational needs, but an organisation managed in this way may not be sustainable over a longer period of time.

Stop and reflect

What management actions can you think of that could lead to employees being demotivated?

What beliefs about human motivation do you think underlie these actions?

What are your own beliefs/assumptions about human motivation?

How do your own assumptions about people affect your behaviour towards others in your work context?

Herzberg's dual-factor theory

Herzberg focuses on work itself as a source of motivation (Herzberg, 1968/ 2003). His views emerged from his research, in the course of which he asked people to recall times when they felt especially satisfied and motivated by their work and times when they felt particularly dissatisfied and demotivated. Employees were also asked to identify what factors had caused these feelings.

Two entirely different sets of factors emerged. For example, a person who listed low pay as a source of dissatisfaction did not necessarily identify high pay as a cause of satisfaction. From this, Herzberg argued that the traditional model of a single dissatisfaction–satisfaction continuum was incorrect in that improvement in some areas (called 'hygiene factors') might help remove dissatisfaction, but would not necessarily increase satisfaction or motivation. Herzberg therefore proposed a dual-factor explanation of motivation. Dual-factor theory refers to two different needs. These are:

1 Hygiene factors, which involve working conditions and can trigger dissatisfaction.

2 Motivator factors, which originate from the nature of the job itself and can create job satisfaction.

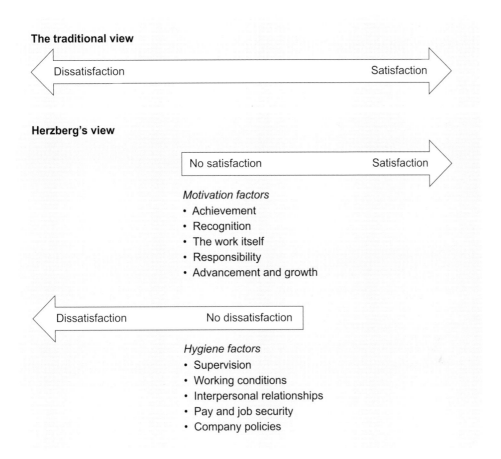

The traditional view

Dissatisfaction   Satisfaction

Herzberg's view

No satisfaction   Satisfaction

Motivation factors
• Achievement
• Recognition
• The work itself
• Responsibility
• Advancement and growth

Dissatisfaction   No dissatisfaction

Hygiene factors
• Supervision
• Working conditions
• Interpersonal relationships
• Pay and job security
• Company policies

Figure 2.2: Herzberg's view of motivation

So, implicit in Herzberg's model is the belief that job satisfaction will lead to higher levels of motivation, while hygiene factors, although they can lead to a state of 'no dissatisfaction', do not act as motivators.

Controversially, in Herzberg's research pay and fringe benefits are classified as hygiene and not motivating factors (a finding probably influenced by the people Herzberg researched, namely professional engineers and managerial staff for whom money may not have been an important motivator). Interestingly, this is an assumption that contradicts Taylor's scientific management approach, which suggested that workers were primarily motivated by monetary incentives. Taylor believed that through methodical study and scientific principles it was possible to establish the one best way of carrying out a task or job.

See the first section of Chapter 1.

For Taylor, applying scientific methods enabled managers to determine the most effective and efficient method of work. He saw his methods as benefitting both worker and manager, since the worker was encouraged to attain his or her peak performance and receive payment in relation to this, but management also obtained increased output. This might be seen as a gross simplification of human motivation, but payment-by-results schemes are still widely used in many organisations.

However, Herzberg's model does seem to offer a crucial insight into people's behaviour at work in concluding that only when a person feels the potential for satisfaction will that person be able to muster significant work motivation. Motivating factors such as responsibility, job challenge, opportunities for achievement or advancement and recognition provide feelings of satisfaction. These factors are associated with job content and are intrinsic or unique to each individual.

Stop and reflect

How far does Herzberg's analysis map onto your experience?

The motivation factors in Figure 2.2 are listed in descending order of importance to Herzberg's interviewees, with achievement being the most important.

Does this match your own experiences?

As with all motivation theories, the model can be criticised. For example, the terms 'satisfaction' and 'motivation' are used as if they are interchangeable, whereas they can potentially mean quite different things (for example, a satisfied need, according to Maslow, no longer motivates). Furthermore, Herzberg's sample of 'two hundred engineers and accountants, who represented a cross section of Pittsburgh industry' (March, 2009, p. 18) is hardly extensive or representative of employees in general. Most seriously, his methodology can be criticised in that people are known to be more likely to attribute positive things to their own efforts, while blaming circumstances outside their control for the negative things – this alone could explain his 'two factors'.

However, Herzberg's theory has been influential in suggesting that:

- satisfaction can be increased by enabling people to take responsibility for what they do and how they do it, and by giving them scope to achieve and advance in their roles
- dissatisfaction can be reduced by having effective organisational policies and procedures, paying workers well, improving the working environment, and so on – but improvement of these factors will not motivate people to work better, except perhaps in the very short term.

In addition, the distinction between motivators and hygiene factors serves to highlight the potentially powerful role of *intrinsic* rewards that derive from the work itself. (You might, however, want to consider whether everyone at work is interested in intrinsic rewards. Perhaps some people *hate* responsibility, satisfy their higher order needs outside work and would prefer a quiet working life for reasonable pay.)

While there are weaknesses in Herzberg's theory, it provides an excellent illustration of how a theory does not have to be perfect to provide a valuable contribution if you concentrate on what is helpful rather than right or wrong with it.

The practical impact of Herzberg's theory can be illustrated by worldwide survey results that highlight the best companies to work for in different sectors as rated by employees – these companies have incorporated both hygiene and motivator factors to create an environment where employees are highly motivated and want to stay (see *The Sunday Times*, 2010, or any number of similar lists).

The implications of Herzberg's **dual-factor theory** for managers are therefore clear. Herzberg suggests that providing hygiene factors will eliminate employee dissatisfaction but will not motivate workers to high achievement levels. So if the challenge is to improve motivation to work, can you as a manager provide an adequate job context of working conditions and benefits for your staff? Can you arouse work interest and promote self-directed task motivation through recognition, challenge and opportunities to learn and advance?

Herzberg suggests that the most effective way to stimulate motivation is through improving the nature of work itself. At the time that Herzberg developed his theory, most jobs were relatively structured and routine (and many still are). Herzberg's idea was that many of these jobs could be enriched – and this is an idea that, when put into practice, has enabled motivation to be built into the design of a job.

Job enrichment

In order to increase the motivation and wellbeing of employees at work, Herzberg advocated the design of jobs so that they can be challenging and more interesting, for example by using employees' talents to a greater degree and giving them more responsibilities. Herzberg called this '**job enrichment**' (the opposite of the **job design** advocated by Taylor's scientific management approach, which suggests that work should be broken down into its simplest and most basic components). Herzberg also distinguished his approach from one in which the number of jobs done by employees is increased (job enlargement) or varied (**job rotation**) (Pugh and Hickson, 2007). Herzberg proposed seven principles of job enrichment (listed in Table 2.1).

Table 2.1: Herzberg's seven principles of job enrichment

Principle	Outcome
1 Remove some controls while retaining accountability	Responsibility and personal achievement
2 Increase the accountability of individuals for their own work	Responsibility and recognition
3 Give a person a complete natural unit of work (for example, module, division, area)	Responsibility, achievement and recognition
4 Grant additional authority to an employee (job freedom)	Responsibility, achievement and recognition
5 Make periodic reports directly available to the worker in person rather than to the supervisor	Internal recognition
6 Introduce new and more difficult tasks not previously handled	Growth and learning
7 Assign individuals specific or specialised tasks, enabling them to become experts	Responsibility, growth and learning

Stop and reflect

Which of Herzberg's principles of job enrichment could you apply to your own team or work context – and how?

What would happen?

How might things change?

In Herzberg's view, well-designed jobs can lead to increased job satisfaction. Employees who have had their work 'enriched' include (according to Herzberg) laboratory technicians, sales representatives and factory supervisors. In all these instances people have felt more job satisfaction and have become more productive, and Herzberg claims that this has led to less supervision and thus in turn has allowed the supervisors to do more interesting, demanding and rewarding work (Pugh and Hickson, 2007).

White spaces
An area not allocated to anyone in particular (from telecommunications – radio frequencies not allocated to a local broadcaster)

Poorly designed jobs, on the other hand, can lead to operations and governance problems by creating overlaps and 'white spaces' between areas of responsibility. Poorly designed jobs are also usually associated with low job satisfaction and poor psychological health. Symptoms can include decreased job performance, increased absenteeism, increased staff turnover, increased accidents, lower organisational commitment, decreased motivation, clinical anxiety and depression. In addition, increased levels of stress can increase the risk of coronary heart disease and cancer. Clearly, the psychological implications of poorly designed jobs are serious both for organisations and for individuals. The implications of some of these problems have led to the commissioning by the UK Department for Business of an in-depth report on employee engagement and its potential benefits for organisations and employees (Macleod and Clarke, 2009).

From the management perspective, however, the implementation of job enrichment is rarely trouble-free, and you will need to think through what you want to do and why carefully. Perhaps the most common cause of the failure of job-enrichment schemes is the lack of commitment of those implementing them. It is very easy to implement a scheme as a reaction rather than as a long-term strategy to improve satisfaction and productivity. Job enrichment is not an easy option, and in most cases the organisation should be prepared for an initial drop in performance as people learn new ways of working. You might experience resistance to change, especially from anxious supervisors or line managers who think their positions are being undermined (one of the ways of minimising adverse reactions is to conduct a small-scale pilot scheme first). If your commitment and the commitment of the staff most directly involved are strong enough, you should be able to convince doubters of the long-term benefits to everyone.

In reading and thinking about these content theories of motivation you may have felt that they have not sufficiently explained why people are motivated to behave in certain ways. You might question whether content theories can be applied in the same way in different parts of the world. Does everyone's psyche work in the same way? Are we all motivated or demotivated by the same factors? Another problem with Herzberg's approach is that it places all of the responsibility on management to determine what kind of work is motivating – the assumption is that managers know how to deliver to employees. Identification of some of the limitations of content theories has led to a greater focus on the processes involved in motivation.

Process theories of motivation

Process theories of motivation are 'a group of theories that explain how employees select behaviours with which to meet their needs and determine whether their choices were successful' (Daft, 2006, p. 704). These theories are called *process* theories because they focus on the mental processes used to evaluate cause-and-effect relationships. As was noted, content theories tend to assume you will be motivated if a job provides rewards or incentives that enable you to meet your needs. The underlying assumption of content theories is therefore that everyone is motivated by the same factors and will behave in similar ways.

But, unfortunately, giving someone a reward may not increase effort and increased effort may not produce better performance. Similarly, people may regard the same job differently, and while some people may perceive work as fulfilling their desire for a particular outcome, others may not. Indeed, that other people may have entirely different desires is an underlying assumption of process theories. What follows is a consideration of some classical process theories: equity theory, expectancy theory and goal theory.

Equity theory

J.S. Adams's equity theory (1963) suggests that motivation is moderated by the perceived fairness of, or discrepancy between, personal contributions and rewards relative to what others receive. One important assumption of this theory is that the less people perceive they get out of work, the less effort they may put into work. According to equity theory, then, a person's perceptions and beliefs about inputs and outcomes are important in judging equity. If there are inequities, people will then act to reduce perceived inequalities in their treatment, for example, by working less or arguing for greater rewards. People look at the linkage between work and outcomes, calculate whether it is fair, and then act accordingly. In practice, however, there are often differences between perceptions, beliefs and reality.

Equity theory also suggests that people hold certain beliefs about the *inputs* and *outcomes* of their jobs. The outcomes of a job include pay, fringe benefits (such as a company car), status, intrinsic interest in the job and any other needs that the person is seeking to satisfy. The inputs are the factors that people perceive they bring to the job – for instance, qualifications and ability, as well as effort and motivation. The theory explains that people add up all their inputs and all their outcomes and compare them to the outcomes and inputs of some other person, or class of people, they perceive to be doing similar work. Where the ratios are equal, equity exists, and people continue to apply the same level of inputs (that is, effort). Equity will exist if any of the following three conditions are met:

- The inputs compared are equal and the outcomes compared are equal.
- The person making the comparisons receives more outcomes for extra inputs.

- The person making the comparisons receives fewer outcomes for fewer inputs.

Where the ratios are unequal, inequity exists, and the person will feel some degree of tension. Inequity can exist if either of the following conditions is met:

- The person making the comparisons receives fewer outcomes for the same or more inputs.
- The person making the comparisons receives more outcomes for the same or fewer inputs.

These relationships are shown in Figure 2.3.

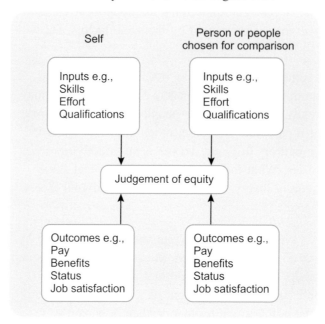

Figure 2.3: Equity theory

Reactions to the tension caused by inequity can take several forms:

- Inputs may be altered.
- Outcomes may be altered.
- Views on inputs and outcomes may be distorted.
- The situation (job) may be left.
- Referenced individuals may be acted upon to change their level of inputs or outcomes.
- The person making the comparisons may start making comparisons with other people.

In each case, the aim of the reaction is to restore a sense of equity. People who perceive others to be gaining more outcomes for less input may reduce their own input, try to persuade their managers to increase the level of outcomes, or try to persuade the others to increase their input or reduce their outcomes.

Equity theory seems to be able to make sensible predictions about people's behaviour and level of motivation when people are *undercompensated* for their work. That is, people will attempt to restore equity when they gain fewer outcomes for the same or more inputs. However, when people are *overcompensated*, the theory makes predictions that diverge from how many people actually behave. Although there is evidence that some people may feel guilty about overcompensation and attempt to restore equity – by, for instance, increasing input – many others find overcompensation quite tolerable, for example, Sir Fred Goodwin the former Chief Executive of The Royal Bank of Scotland did not see anything wrong with a reported award of a pension of £16 million from a bank that had posted huge losses under his leadership. Therefore, while it seems true that the less people get out of work, the less likely they are to be motivated, it does not always follow that the more people get out of work, the more they put into it.

Although equity theory cannot fully explain motivation, the theory gives rise to a number of important managerial principles. The first is that people will and do make comparisons with others at work, and perceived inequity can lead to a loss of satisfaction and decreased motivation. As a manager you should be sensitive to this comparison process and try to ensure, where possible and desirable, that such comparisons do not lead to perceived inequity. The second principle is that equity and inequity are perceived, not absolute, concepts. In this respect, managers should be sensitive to the perspectives of others in order to avoid perceived inequity.

Expectancy theory

Motivation and performance are highest when **valence**, **instrumentality** and **expectancy** are all high (Vroom, 1964). That is, people will increase their effort when effort is seen to be linked directly to job performance (expectancy), and job performance to rewards (instrumentality), and the rewards are the ones that *matter* to those involved (valence). Rewards that are not guaranteed by increased job performance can act as motivators, as long as individuals believe that by exerting effort they can *increase the likelihood* of obtaining the reward (for example, the sales bonus on reaching the sales target). Rewards that come anyway, regardless of the effort put in, are not likely to act as motivators.

Thus, expectancy theory highlights some important issues of management that are worth considering:

- Ability – a manager must establish whether the person is capable of the required performance.
- Goals – if effort is to be linked to performance, clear, agreed and measurable goals are needed and regular feedback on performance should be given. Unfortunately, this is not easy, as goals may be difficult to measure, there may be genuine disagreements about them, or they may be ambiguous.
- Resources – the resources required to do a job include appropriate tools, materials and equipment, and the necessary information. If any of these are lacking, people will feel that the level of performance they achieve does not depend solely on their efforts. Instead, it is limited by factors outside their control. This will tend to reduce motivation.
- Time – this is another major factor that will limit performance. Performance will be limited by having more to do than is possible in the available time. This may be one factor within a manager's control when allocating work to others. It is useful to give people as much notice as

possible. If deadlines are clearly specified, a person can then allocate time between the various tasks in the most efficient way.

- Job design – this influences the link between effort and performance.

It is unlikely that either equity theory or expectancy theory could give complete explanations of your own levels of motivation, or of those of other people. However, it is likely that both equity theory and expectancy theory do go some way to explaining motivation. It is also likely that, when thinking of other people's attitudes and perceptions, you will be able to explain some of their levels of motivation. It is therefore important to make sure not only that in reality there is equity, and that the links between effort, performance and rewards are strong, but also that people perceive this to be so. However, if you try to convince people that equity exists and that effort, performance and rewards are linked when they are not, people will eventually learn from their own experience that they have been deceived. The result of this deception may be a short-term increase in motivation, but it could result in a lasting decrease in motivation over the longer term.

Goals drive motivation: Goal-setting theory

Goal-setting theory is another process theory and highlights the importance of the goals that people actually set themselves to fulfil their needs as the driver of their motivations.

Goal-setting theory was developed by Edwin Locke and Gary Latham (1969), who proposed that specific, challenging goals increase motivation and performance when the goals are accepted by people and if they receive feedback to indicate their progress toward goal achievement (Daft, 2006, p. 708). The main premise of goal-setting theory is that people's goals or intentions play an important part in determining behaviour (Mullins, 2008). People set their goals and attempt to achieve them in a manner that is concordant with their needs and values. In trying to achieve these goals, people notice the consequences of their behaviour. If it seems likely that goals they have set are not going to be achieved by their current behaviour, they can either modify their goals to make them more realistic or modify their behaviour in order to achieve the goal. Goal-setting theory includes the following components:

- 'Goal specificity' refers to the degree to which goals are real and unambiguous, which is necessary in order to direct behaviour and maintain motivation.

- 'Goal difficulty' suggests that hard goals are more motivating than easy ones but that they should be achievable. Effort increases when the person is committed to attaining the goal.

- 'Goal acceptance' requires that employees must 'buy into' the goals and become committed to them.

- 'Feedback' refers to continued dialogue about the progress being made towards achieving the goals. The agenda for this is often set by management.

Think about a job with which you are familiar. Can you think of three or more ways in which goal-setting theory could be used to increase the motivation of people within that job?

Goal-setting theory tells us how to set goals, but not which goals to set. Setting goals can involve negotiation between people, as managers try to ensure employees' own goals are consistent with those of the organisation.

You may have thought of several ways of improving motivation. Goal-setting theory indicates that motivation can be improved in the following ways:

- Setting challenging, but realistic, goals. Goals that are too difficult will lead to decreased performance, especially over the longer term.
- Setting clearly understood goals, with specific performance targets. Unclear and vague goals are just as bad as setting no goals whatsoever.
- Supplying complete, timely and accurate feedback. This enables people to see clearly and quickly how their own behaviour can be changed to improve performance.

Goal-setting theory goes one step further than content theories, in that it attempts to link motivation directly to job performance. Although goal-setting theory provides a different explanation of motivation from that of value theories, none of these theories can be used independently of the others to provide a full explanation of motivation. A consideration of people's needs will help explain their values, and their values will help explain their preferred goals and their commitment to those goals. Thus, as a manager, it is important to keep all these theories in mind when trying to assess how to improve motivation. Together, they will enable you to answer the questions posed near the beginning of this section:

- How do you make it possible for members of your team to gain desired goals through good job performance?
- How do you make it possible for members of your team to gain desired goals repeatedly – so as to maintain their good job performance?

2.2: Teams and groups

There have always been tasks too great for one person to tackle alone, such as early tribes hunting large animals, and today, for example, a task as simple as producing a local newsletter will require people to write articles, organise its printing and deliver it around the area. There are also large, multifaceted tasks such as organising the Olympic Games in London or the football World Cup in South Africa, both of which involve complex funding, infrastructure and logistical issues to develop and deliver over a number of years to tight timescales. Coordination of effort and delegation of responsibility is all part of getting things done. The ability to manage teams and understand how teams work is an important component of managerial and organisational success.

Many organisations have adopted a **matrix-structure** to promote cross-functional working across different disciplines and expertise. These are often 'temporary' groups, brought together to achieve a particular project and then disbanded. One challenge that often faces managers is the variable performance of teams – why is it that some teams seem to work very effectively whereas others have huge conflicts and problems within them? This section will look at the way teams work and the behaviours that can contribute to their success or failure. An understanding of these areas can help you to evaluate your own team performance and identify any necessary changes.

A frequent challenge for managers, as you will by now be well aware, is the tension between rational aspects of a task, such as planning and coordinating activities, and those aspects that go beyond the purely rational into more psychological, subjective and, therefore, emotive aspects, such as creative team spirit. This tension is particularly important in considering the development of groups and teams. A team will usually have been formed to undertake a specific task, but its success in this may depend on the interpersonal dynamics within the team. Therefore, the job of developing a team and managing its dynamics requires as much attention as managing the more overt and rational aspects of the task. This section will address both the rational, task-focused dimension of team-working and the interpersonal and process-focused aspects.

While teams can be an extremely effective way of organising work, the same features that make a group effective can sometimes result in 'team pathologies' – ways in which a group can be seriously *ineffective*. This section will address some of the more common dangers associated with group working and suggest some creative ways of both building teams and helping to surface and resolve problems. It will also look at some challenges for teams, in particular working across organisational boundaries in virtual and international settings.

A relatively simple model of managing both team tasks and group dynamics was developed by the US managerial psychologists Blake and Mouton (1964). They proposed two fundamental ingredients of managerial behaviour:

> One is concern for production: the other is concern for people. 'Concern for' does not mean a dedication for specific targets, nor does it mean the results achieved in themselves. It means the general approach.

> (Source: Pugh and Hickson, 1989, p. 162)

Usually today the two approaches are called 'task focussed' and 'people focussed'. A manager who is entirely task focussed neglects the human aspects, such as group dynamics. The manager may be successful in the short term, but is unlikely to promote staff development, initiative or empowerment. This manager is likely to be following McGregor's Theory X, as discussed earlier in the chapter.

On the other hand, a manager who is entirely people focussed neglects the coordination of staff effort. So the tasks, if and when achieved, whether in production or services, may not be of excellent quality.

Obviously most people are not at either extreme, but can tend towards one approach or the other, whereas the model suggests that the ideal manager needs to combine both approaches and integrate them appropriately according to their staff and the situation.

Groups or teams?

Although the terms 'groups' and 'teams' are often used interchangeably, first of all it is necessary to examine what is meant by each. Essentially a team is a particular kind of group, so it is helpful to understand what is meant by a group before embarking on a discussion of particular issues surrounding teams.

Types and uses of groups

It is difficult to define the concept of a group precisely. The essential features are that it has two or more members who are aware of each other, interact and work towards a common goal and with the outcome less dependent on whether there is a contribution from all the members. However, this definition could apply to a collection of neighbours chatting in the street, a small crowd or a queue waiting at a bus stop. Schein (1980, p. 137) suggests that another important ingredient of a group is that the people 'perceive themselves to be a group'. Thus, neighbours may come together to form a group to pursue a common interest – for example, a neighbourhood watch or support of a local football team. Groups are generally fairly small, often developing a distinct identity, which may be reflected in a name, rituals, territory, and so on.

Neighbourhood watch
A community initiative set up to encourage local residents in the same area to watch their neighbours' property in an attempt to reduce crime in that area

There are various types of groups within organisations. Kakabadse et al. (1988) have suggested a useful categorisation: groups may be formal or informal, primary or secondary (see Figure 2.4).

	Formal	Informal
Primary	e.g., department, project team	e.g., group of friends
Secondary	e.g., large committee	e.g., a network of computer enthusiasts or women managers

Figure 2.4: Different types of groups

- Formal groups have some formal recognition and authority within the organisation and usually have a defined purpose or task that is related to the overall task of the organisation. They might be departments, work groups or project teams. An organisation can be regarded as consisting of an interlocking set of such work groups.

- Informal groups do not have formal authority. Individuals within organisations interact with a wide range of other people who may not be part of their formal groups. They may form relationships with those people to pursue common interests, or to make various exchanges. Informal groups may form to fulfil special needs and goals – to provide friendship, a sense of identity and belonging, or to pursue a common interest such as sport. For example, a mixture of city bankers and lawyers who were lifelong Manchester United Football Club fans in the UK got together a bid to buy the club (Gibson, 2010). Informal groups may also form to pursue work-related interests.

- Primary groups are those whose members have regular and frequent interactions with each other in the pursuit of some common interests or tasks. A small work group, project team or family are all primary groups. They usually have an important influence on their members' values, attitudes and beliefs.

- Secondary groups are those whose members interact less frequently. A large committee, a professional group or an association are all examples. They are often larger than primary groups and their members may not have the opportunity to get to know each other well. As a result, secondary groups are usually less cohesive than primary groups.

Formal groups are used for a variety of functions in organisations, especially those requiring a combination of different skills, knowledge, perspectives or interests. These functions may include:

- distributing and managing work
- problem solving and decision making
- passing on information
- coordinating and liaising
- enabling people to participate in decision making
- negotiation or conflict resolution
- inquests or inquiries into the past.

Although informal groups, by their very nature, rarely have clearly defined organisational purposes, they may also serve some of the functions outlined. For example, a group of staff members who meet regularly to play badminton may serve also as a channel for passing on information, or to discuss past events and problems.

A common source of difficulties with groups arises when the same group is expected to perform two different functions simultaneously. For example, a management meeting that starts as a negotiation between departments is unlikely to proceed satisfactorily to a discussion of the long-term plans of the organisation. Thus, the functions of groups need to be clearly separated, perhaps by time, place, title or a change of style. For example, a committee might find it useful to separate the part of a meeting dealing with administrative matters from that part dealing with future plans, and to adopt a different style for each part. The committee could adopt a fairly brisk and formal style to deal with routine administration, have a break, and then choose a more relaxed and participative style to deal with future plans. It could take this separation even further and have occasional review days offsite to discuss plans in more detail.

Individuals, too, may use groups to serve a variety of different needs and interests. Some of the main categories are summarised below.

Individuals' benefits from belonging to groups

1 Satisfying social needs

2 Establishing or confirming an identity

3 Gaining help and support in carrying out their particular objectives (which may not be the same as the organisation's)

4 Sharing and helping in a common activity

(Source: adapted from Handy, 1976, p. 147)

Any group can be regarded as working at two levels: the level of the task (tackling the business of the group) and the social level (meeting people's needs for acceptance, recognition, belonging, and so on). So working in a group is both a task and a social process. These two aspects of a group are interrelated: people are unlikely to contribute effectively to the group task if they are feeling uncomfortable, threatened or anxious; and people are unlikely to feel happy and comfortable in a group unless they think that the group's task is being tackled in a reasonable manner. Both aspects of a group are important for its effectiveness.

Improving group effectiveness

An effective group is one that achieves its agreed aims and enables its members to derive satisfaction from their work in the group. This sub-section will examine some of the main factors that influence the effectiveness of formal groups. These factors can be divided into two sorts. Contextual factors or 'givens' are the first sort – these are factors that usually have to be negotiated with other people in the organisation outside the group. They include the *size* and *composition* of the group, the *task* it is to accomplish, the *resources* it has at its disposal and the *external recognition* it receives from other groups in the organisation. Once established, these factors often take some time to change and may be regarded as 'givens' or constraints within which the group will operate.

The second group of factors is internal or intervening factors. These are factors that are more under the direct control of group members and can therefore, in theory at least, be changed within a relatively short timescale to improve group performance. They include *leadership*, *task* and *maintenance* functions, *interaction patterns*, *motivation* and *group development*.

Contextual factors or 'givens'

Group size

Many committees delegate specific tasks or projects to small groups of two to four people. The size of a group will depend in part on the nature of the task being addressed. For example, a stakeholder engagement group in a company may have to be quite large to represent all the different interests, whereas a team set up to examine ways of re-organising the reception area might be quite small. The larger the group is, the greater the diversity of skills and knowledge available to it. Yet at the same time, the larger the group, the less opportunity there is for each individual to participate and influence proceedings. The size of the group is therefore a trade-off. Research shows that in order to enable all members to participate effectively, a group of between five and seven people is best, but to achieve the range of expertise and skills required, it may need to be larger. As a group increases beyond, say, ten or twelve people it may become less effective and perhaps may tend to split into smaller sub-groups.

Group composition

In deciding the composition of a group it is important to have members with the necessary competencies to tackle the group task. However, other considerations are important, too. *Homogeneous* groups, whose members share similar values and beliefs, tend to produce higher member satisfaction and less conflict, yet they tend to be less creative and produce greater pressures for conformity. *Heterogeneous* groups, in contrast, are likely to experience greater conflict, but have the potential for greater creativity and innovation. As the heterogeneous group members have a wider range of views and opinions, their decisions are also more likely to be widely accepted within the organisation. A successful implementation of diversity policies will lead to organisations employing people with a greater range of experiences, backgrounds, etc., as a result of which, groups will probably become more heterogeneous.

Such diverse groupings can occur, for example, in partnerships between public sector and community groups where people are invited to represent the community in government planning. However, once invited, they may find that there is little recognition of their differing experiences and skills in a formal meeting setting. Groups can also become transnational and cross-cultural, working in virtual teams across national boundaries. This is becoming more prevalent as a result of advances in information technology and the globalisation of business. It is inevitable that increasing the diversity of a group may also increase the potential for disagreement, and dealing with tensions and conflicts is an important topic that will be considered later in this book.

The nature of the task

A group that is given a task that it feels is *realistic* and *important* is more likely to perform better than one that is not. Some tasks may require very different forms of group behaviour and will be difficult to do together. For example, a group formed to disseminate information may not be the best place for attempting creative problem solving as well. Probably it is best not to give one group such 'conflicting' tasks, and if they are, the tasks need to be clearly separated in some way, perhaps by dealing with them in separate meetings.

Ideally the task should contain the right degree of *challenge* for the group. A task that is too difficult may lead to failure and damage morale. A task that is too easy will leave the group with little sense of challenge or accomplishment when the task is complete. In most cases, a group that is given a clear and unambiguous task can perform more quickly than one that is given an open-ended and ambiguous task. Clearly, not all tasks can be well defined, however. Groups given ill-defined tasks will probably need more support and members who can tolerate greater stress. They will also need to be allowed more time to become an effective group.

Resources and support
For a group to function effectively, it will need adequate resources. The people establishing the group will need access to the necessary equipment, finance and support services to do the job. One of the quickest ways of reducing group morale and effectiveness is to deprive it of the resources it needs to function smoothly!

External recognition

> No one wants to spend whole mornings in committees whose conclusions will never be noticed, or will be overruled.

> (Handy, 1999)

The standing of a group and its members in the wider organisation will also affect group productivity and morale. If members feel that the work of their group or committee is accepted as being important to the organisation and contributing to its goals then they are more likely to be motivated. Equally, the group will need to be clear how its results will be reported to the rest of the organisation. Again, the morale of the group is likely to diminish if it feels it cannot communicate relevant findings from its work to the rest of the organisation.

Internal or intervening factors
Internal factors are the aspects of group work that can be controlled directly by the group itself and can be modified in the short term, taking account of the contextual factors to improve group performance or satisfaction.

Leadership
The way in which leadership is exercised needs to be appropriate to the circumstances faced by the group and to be acceptable to the group's members if the group is to perform well.

Task and maintenance functions
As was mentioned earlier, a group functions at two levels. To be effective a group needs to be able not only to tackle the task in hand but also to maintain social relations within the group itself. Effective groups must therefore carry out **task functions** and **maintenance functions**.

Task functions include ensuring that the group shares a common understanding of the task in hand, problem solving, initiating structures to enable the task to be attained, and controlling the activities of a group to achieve its goal. The specific task functions that are needed will vary according to the nature of the task.

Some common task functions are described in Table 2.2.

Table 2.2: Common task functions

Proposing/initiating	Proposing ideas, courses of action that are relevant to the task
Building	Developing other people's proposals
Diagnosing	Analysing what is wrong or what is the cause of a particular situation
Giving and seeking information	Offering and seeking information that is relevant to the task
Evaluating	Evaluating the merits of particular proposals and outcomes
Decision making	Contributing to decisions on a particular proposal or course of action

All of these functions will probably be involved in any task that involves problem solving. It is worth noting that groups tackling problems in a considered and systematic way are likely to be more effective than those attempting to 'muddle through'. Groups frequently jump too quickly from initial proposals to opinion-seeking to evaluation and decision making, without exploring the problem or systematically examining a range of possible solutions. Problem solving is also about dealing with conflict in groups so that the group's efforts remain constructive rather than destructive.

Maintenance functions help to maintain the morale and harmony of a group and create an atmosphere in which people feel they can work together productively. In part this is about trying to meet people's needs for inclusion, control, affection and respect. Some common maintenance functions are listed in Table 2.3.

Table 2.3: Common maintenance functions

Gate-keeping	Opening – positively attempting to involve others in discussion
	Closing – attempting to control or cut off others
Encouraging	Being friendly, supportive and responsive to other people by verbal or non-verbal means
Conflict resolution	Being prepared to acknowledge and deal with conflict
Giving feedback	Giving positive feedback on people's contributions
Dealing with feelings	Recognising and acknowledging people's feelings
Looking after physical needs	Meeting people's physical needs in the group, for example, by providing adequate amenities, refreshments, etc.

A common tendency among people and groups is to give inadequate attention to maintenance functions – to believe that the task is really the only thing that matters. While the task is obviously important, a group is unlikely to be effective for long if it denies maintenance functions. People will probably find the group provides a poor environment in which to work, destructive conflicts may develop and morale will fall.

Interaction patterns

Another factor that the group itself can control is the pattern of interaction or communication between members. The most common patterns are shown in Figure 2.5.

In the 'wheel' pattern all communication in the group is channelled through one person, usually the manager or leader of the group. In the 'all-channel' pattern, anyone can communicate directly with anyone else in the group.

Experiments using these patterns have shown that:

- the wheel pattern is always the quickest to reach a solution or conclusion
- in dealing with complex open-ended problems, the all-channel pattern is the most likely to reach the best solution; with the wheel pattern, the abilities of the central person will determine the pattern's effectiveness
- the level of satisfaction for individuals is fairly high in the all-channel pattern and mixed in the wheel pattern, the central figure expressing greater satisfaction and those at the outlying positions feeling more isolated.

Chairs of meetings need to be aware of this last point.

Under pressure of time or competition the all-channel pattern is likely to restructure itself into a wheel, or disintegrate. In general, wheel patterns are good for speedy results where quality is not vital, but morale may be low for all but the leader. All-channel patterns are participative and produce good

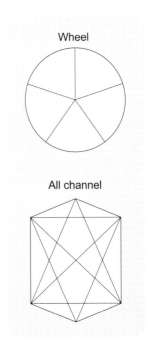

Wheel

All channel

Figure 2.5: 'Wheel' and 'all-channel' patterns of communication

quality results, but they take time and do not stand up so well under pressure. It is a question of using the right pattern for the right task.

Motivation

Motivation is an important aspect of working in groups and there are certain aspects that need to be stressed here in relation to groups:

1   Motivation is more than satisfaction, which is one possible outcome of groups. Lack of satisfaction can lead to absenteeism and turnover of members. But a satisfied group is not necessarily a productive group.

2   Knowledge of expected results, together with a belief that what is expected is realistic, will help to motivate the individuals in a group. Information on how performance actually compares with expectations is also required. These factors are as vital to the motivation of groups as they are for individuals.

3   Motivation by involving people in decisions affecting the group will only work if the group and the task are important enough to the individual to justify acceptance of additional responsibility and any other costs.

4   Perhaps the most important aspect of motivation in groups is a mission or set of goals that is highly valued by the group's members. In the absence of such a mission, group members are more likely to put their own individual goals and interests before those of the group. Group coherence and performance may also improve when the group perceives some external threat or competitor as a 'common enemy' of the group, though there is a danger of 'groupthink' (discussed later) in such a situation.

Teams and what they offer

A team is more than a group. When you think of all the groups to which you belong, you will probably find that very few of them are really teams. A team is a special sort of group with the following characteristics:

- It has a common goal or task to pursue.
- The pursuit of this goal or task requires collaboration and the coordination of activities among the team's members.
- The team members have regular and frequent interactions with each other.
- It has a team identity, which is distinct from its members' individual identities.

Some common types of teams

Teams may be established for different reasons and can take a variety of forms. Teams are frequently established to tackle particular, *discrete tasks*. Small task teams are frequently set up to develop new strategies or policies in a particular area, and these teams are sometimes called working parties or task forces.

Teams may be established around a particular *function*. For example, a group of department heads may form the senior management team. Location is another basis on which teams develop. Close collaboration and coordination of work can occur between people sharing the same location. This is quite common when a national organisation has several offices in different parts of the country. However, collaboration and coordination can also occur when people just happen to work in the same room or the same part of a building if there is a shared goal or task, because this is an important determinant of whether a team exists or whether it does not.

Teams are also formed to undertake particular *projects*. Project teams are normally established for a specific time and have a defined task or target to achieve. Project teams are usually distinguished from task teams by lasting over a longer term and having at least some workers who commit a high proportion or all of their working time to the project. Project teams may also have a higher degree of autonomy from the work of the rest of the organisation.

Working in teams has advantages, for example:

- the chance to bring a variety of skills and experiences to tackling a problem or task
- the opportunity for people to learn from each other
- mutual support
- the potential for team members to enthuse and motivate each other
- a degree of independence from the rest of the organisation.

Team-working may also have disadvantages, even when the team is working well, for example, there can be:

- too much isolation from the rest of the organisation, leading to goals being out of tune with organisational goals
- team pressures, leading to an unrealistic view of the world (groupthink)
- competition between teams, leading to conflict.

Of course, if the team is not working well, there may also be other disadvantages.

'Team' is not a neutral word. As Parsloe (1981) observed, it is 'soaked in positive values'. Teams are expected to be collaborative, egalitarian, cooperative and committed. Our images of teams are so positive that the word 'team' is often used to describe any arrangement in which staff are nominally grouped together, irrespective of whether they actually work together as a team. In fact, groups that do not work collaboratively may be called teams, perhaps to hide this fact, or in the hope that greater collaboration will result. Stanton (1989) reviewed the findings of research on team-working in the personal social services and concluded that 'loud and sustained calls for better team-working are a signal of its absence'.

All this means that you need to be careful when you see or hear the word 'team'. Just because something is called a team does not mean that it actually works like one.

Managing a team

When creating a team, managers often select on the basis of the skills needed, but it is also important to think about the roles and functions that people in the team need to perform. A number of psychologists have developed frameworks that help people to identify the roles they prefer to play in teams. Perhaps the best known, and one you may have come across, is Meredith Belbin's team roles (1981, 1993). He identifies nine roles:

- The 'coordinator', who establishes the goals, allocates roles and responsibilities, is assertive, conscientious and has drive.

- The 'plant', who advances new ideas and strategies with attention to major issues. This person is often imaginative and intelligent, but may resent criticism and be careless of detail.

- The 'implementer', who converts ideas and objectives into practical operational procedures and who is task-oriented, conscientious and affiliative.

- The 'monitor evaluator', who analyses rather than creates ideas. The monitor evaluator's main contribution is the ability to find weaknesses in what is going on, even though sometimes these could be issues that are remote to the team (but necessary to it).

- The 'shaper', who shapes the way in which team effort is applied, directs others attention to the team's priorities and objectives. The shaper imposes order on group discussions and the activities, often appearing aggressive at times.

- The 'team-worker', who is most concerned with harmony within the team and who is most supportive and understanding of other team members. The team-worker is likeable, popular, uncompetitive, which makes this person tend not to be noticed except when absent.

- The 'resource investigator', who is an extroverted, stable member who identifies ideas and resources in the external environment. The resource investigator's enthusiasm might not be maintained throughout the team's task, however.

- The 'completer finisher', who identifies areas that need more work and looks for possible omissions. The completer finisher can be anxious about detail and often has high standards and likes to push to complete the task on time.

- The 'specialist', who provides specialist knowledge and skills. The specialist is often single-minded and self-motivating.

Belbin's model provides a way of describing the team roles required for team work to be successful. He suggests that a team works best if there is:

- a match between an individual's responsibilities and his or her 'natural' team role

- diversity in members' mental abilities

- an ability to identify and adjust imbalances in the group

- a strong plant to produce ideas for the team

- a good coordinator to show patience and command, seek out ability and elicit trust

- a range of team roles available to the group.

Managers and practitioners have used his model widely, but it is not the only model of successful teams. Different team roles are important at different stages of a group's life. Although Belbin's roles do shed some light on preferences within a team, some people do not feel very comfortable with their categorisation, as some roles seem much more exciting than others, and there has been limited empirical support for using this model. Belbin's work has been criticised by Fincham and Rhodes (2005) who suggest that:

- the nature of assigning an individual to his or her team role is problematic
- the measures of team roles have poor reliability and validity, and thus roles are sometimes over-interpreted
- the role types are seen as being fixed, rigid attributes of individuals, and this can encourage labelling of individuals
- caution is required to avoid placing too much emphasis on team role specifics.

There are also issues about the extent to which Belbin's ideas travel across cultures.

Some psychologists, using the ideas of Carl Jung (1875–1961), have developed a sixteenfold categorisation of team roles. The first of these is the Myers-Briggs Type Indicator (MBTi), and more recently another psychologist (also called Myers but not related) has developed and refined the Myers-Briggs model to show how different preferences come together to create the ingredients of a team. This is called the Management Team Roles Indicator (MTR-i) (Berens et al., 2004). Whereas the MBTi focuses on instinctively preferred behaviours, the MTR-i focuses on more transient aspects of personality.

When Jung's four preferences (Sensing, Intuition, Thinking and Feeling) are combined with the two orientations (extraversion and introversion), the result is the eight team roles measured by the Management Team Role Indicator (MTRi™) which is part of the Type Mapping™ system. An overview of the MTR-i™ team roles is given in Table 2.4.

Table 2.4: Overview of the MTR-i™ team roles

Jungian Function	Inner World	Outer World
Feeling	**Campaigning (Feeling directed inwardly)** When someone is Campaigning, they give importance to particular thoughts, ideas, or beliefs. The mental process of campaigning is value driven, and in a team discussion Campaigning often brings a sense of priority that is derived from strong convictions. Campaigning seizes upon and emphasises ideas or thoughts that have the greatest import, bringing them to the fore and stressing their significance. Campaigning evaluates the inherent value or importance of new ideas, focusing on those that stimulate the strongest feelings.	**Harmonising (Feeling directed outwardly)** When someone is Harmonising, they try to create harmony in the world around them, by building rapport with people, creating a positive team atmosphere, looking after people's welfare, motivating people and/or providing a service to the satisfaction of others. Harmonising values people's contributions, seeks to develop the role that others play, and invests a lot of effort in building positive relationships. Harmonising tries to overcome differences of opinion and find ways in which the team can agree.
Intuition	**Innovating (Intuition directed inwardly)** When someone is Innovating they use their imagination to create radically new and different ideas or perspectives. Innovating delves into the vast pool of ever-changing ideas and images that exist within the unconscious mind, producing radical solutions to problems, a long-term vision and an apparent understanding of the unknown. Innovating also involves observing the world, but using the imagination to consider what is observed from a number of alternative perspectives.	**Exploring (Intuition directed outwardly)** When someone is Exploring, they try out new and better ways of doing things, to uncover hidden potential in people, things or situations. They break new ground, and are often looking one step beyond the current situation to pursue unexplored avenues, until all the possibilities have been exhausted. Exploring often challenges the status quo whilst experimenting with the introduction of change, to see if the situation can be improved or new potential uncovered.
Sensing	**Clarifying (Sensing directed inwardly)** When someone is Clarifying, they are bringing clarity to the inner world of information, ideas and understanding. Clarifying involves listening, asking questions and absorbing information, to achieve as clear a picture or understanding as is possible. Clarifying involves expanding knowledge, collecting experiences, and looking to the foreseeable future by envisaging clear goals and clear pathways to achievement of those goals. The focus on clarity also brings greater attention to detail.	**Activating (Sensing directed outwardly)** When someone is Activating they are bringing things to fruition by getting things done, and getting them done now! Activating is very action-oriented, dealing with whatever tasks the current situation presents, and spurring others into action as well. Activating makes use of experience and utilises tools or processes that are readily available or tried and trusted. Activating has an immediate impact on things, injecting a sense of urgency, and aiming to achieve clear goals and high-quality, tangible results.
Thinking	**Analysing (Thinking directed inwardly)** When someone is analysing, they produce explanations of how and why things happen. Analysing brings structure and organisation into the inner world of ideas and understanding. It involves formulating hypotheses and explanations of how things function, and gathering evidence to assess how true those explanations are. Analysing also produces mental models that replicate how particular aspects of the world work, and tries to understand the full complexity of any situation.	**Conducting (Thinking directed outwardly)** When someone is Conducting, they introduce organisation and a logical structure into the way things are done. Conducting involves organising and systematising the world, establishing appropriate plans, identifying and implementing the correct procedures, and then endeavouring to make sure they are followed. Conducting tries to ensure that roles and responsibilities are properly defined and that appropriate resources or skills are available to undertake the work assigned.

(Source: Myers, 2010)

2: Working with people

It can be really good for team development for members of a team each to go through these roles as a team-building exercise.

High performing teams

How to combine these different roles into effective and high performing teams both within and across organisational boundaries is an issue that concerns many in managerial roles. In the 1960s, Bruce Tuckman developed a theory of the stages of team development that he thought all teams went through (Tuckman, 1965).

He suggests that groups go through four stages: 'forming', 'storming', 'norming' and 'performing', which can be summarised as follows.

1 Forming – at this stage the group is not fully a group but rather a collection of individuals. It is characterised by general talk about the purpose, identity, composition, lifespan, leadership and working arrangements of the group. Individuals are usually keen to make an impression on the group and establish their own personal identities.

2 Storming – most groups go through a period of conflict after an initial superficial consensus. At this stage, the purpose, leadership and other roles, working patterns and behaviour of the group or of its members may all be challenged. People's individual goals, or 'personal agendas', may be revealed during this process and some interpersonal conflict is to be expected. This stage is particularly important in the formation of trust within the group – people are testing out each other and the group, and revealing more about themselves. If successfully handled, this stage leads to the formulation of more realistic goals and procedures.

3 Norming – this stage is characterised by the group establishing the norms and patterns of work under which it will operate, for example, how it should work, how decisions are taken and what degree of openness, trust and confidence are appropriate between members. There will probably be much tentative experimentation by people who are testing feelings and opinions within the group and establishing their level of commitment.

4 Performing – only when the previous three stages have been completed will the group be fully productive. Although some level of performance will have been achieved during earlier phases, output will have been diminished by the energy put into resolving the group processes and exploring individual objectives and roles. In many committees and groups that meet infrequently, the basic issues of objectives, procedures and appropriate leadership patterns are never fully resolved, and may continue to hinder the group, often leading to frustration and reduced effectiveness.

Tuckman later added a fifth stage, 'adjourning', which recognises that groups and teams often disband or re-form into other groupings once a task has been completed, and it is necessary to recognise the characteristics of this stage as well (Tuckman and Jensen, 1977). People may be feeling uncertain about the future. They may be experiencing stress in the transition from one group setting to another, in parting from the group or in having nothing specific to move on to. Managers can help here by giving supportive feedback on past performance and by encouraging people to continue networking with former colleagues in the group. Social events to mark the end of the work of a group are valuable, too, not only as a way of marking the transition, but in interpersonal terms as well.

However, more recent research by Knight (2006) examines Tuckman's ideas and suggests that, much though his stages are used, they are not necessarily experienced by all teams. In particular, Knight found that very few teams followed the Tuckman model, although they did follow a variant of this. In particular, groups did not progress through the model in a linear way. Forming, norming and performing occurred alongside each other at 25 per cent of completing the task, norming at 40 per cent and performing at 45 per cent. Very little storming was observed. One area of work where effective team performance is often a life or death issue is the military, so it is not surprising that much research in this area has been conducted for the armed forces. Knight's work was conducted in this setting, so it may be that these were highly disciplined teams. However, Tuckman himself observed little storming but explained this away by the artificial nature of the task in his own experiments.

 Stop and reflect

Thinking about the team role preferences in your own team(s), try explaining why the team might have problems functioning effectively as a team? What are the positive factors that help your team to function well?

Teams working virtually and across boundaries

A key facet of team-working nowadays is that teams are dispersed across both organisational and, often, national boundaries. Two types of teams that are increasingly being used are virtual teams and global teams. The formation of virtual teams allows organisations to draw talent quickly from different functions, locations and organisations (Duarte and Snyder, 2006). These approaches to team work have become possible through advances in information technology. Virtual teams can communicate from great distances or be part of a group that works in the same building (Duarte and Snyder, 2006). They rely on technology to make up for the lack of face-to-face meeting and use email, voicemail, videoconferencing, internet and intranet technologies and various types of collaboration software to perform their work, although they might sometimes meet face to face (Daft, 2006). Virtual teams present several unique challenges for managers. Daft (2006, p. 775) suggests the following critical issues:

- *Selecting the right team members.* The first step is creating a team of people who have the right mix of technical and interpersonal skills, task knowledge and personalities to work in a virtual environment.

- *Managing socialisation.* People need to get to know one another and understand the appropriate behaviours and attitudes.

- *Fostering trust.* An essential ingredient, as teams that exhibit high levels of trust tend to have clear roles and expectations of one another, get to know one another as individuals, and maintain positive action-orientated attitudes.

- *Effectively managing communications*. While frequent communication is essential, managers or team leaders need to understand when and how to use various forms of communication to best advantage.

Virtual teams are also sometimes global teams. Govindarajan and Gupta (2001, p. 63) define global teams as 'a cross-border team of individuals of different nationalities, working in different cultures, businesses and functions, who come together to coordinate some aspect of the multinational operation on a global basis' These types of teams also place challenges on managers to make them successful. Bringing people together from different nations means that they come with different values and beliefs, as well as the challenges of bridging gaps of time, distance and culture (Daft, 2006). Examples of challenges might include members speaking different languages, different technologies and different ideas about team work itself. Their success requires investment in resources and adequate time in preparation and orientation of the members at the beginning of the task.

Stop and reflect

How well do virtual teams operate in your own organisation?

Common problems in groups and teams

When a great deal of effort has gone into building a team, it can seem counter-productive to disband it and start over again with a new team for a new project. However, teams that have been together for a long time can develop problems that prevent them working together as effectively as they might. So, it is worth focusing on some of the common ways in which groups 'go wrong'. For example, the group may be too large, its goal may be unrealistic, it may have the wrong people involved and it may not have developed successfully. However, there are several other problems that do not fit so readily into the categories discussed so far. Four will be discussed here:

- hidden agendas
- blind spots
- group anxiety
- 'groupthink'.

Hidden agendas and blind spots

In attempting to understand group dynamics it is important to recognise that levels of 'self-awareness' between members of a group will differ. An individual will be aware of things that other members of the group are not aware of and vice versa. As we saw earlier, individuals bring their own objectives to groups. Things that an individual wants or expects from the group that the group does not know about are called **hidden agendas**.

Common examples of hidden agendas include:

- someone using a meeting to impress another colleague
- someone resisting a proposal on spurious grounds because that person is not prepared to reveal the real reasons behind the resistance

- someone using a meeting to embarrass or 'put down' another member of the group for personal reasons.

The best way to handle hidden agendas is often to bring them into the open early on – at the storming stage of group development. For example, the group might have a round robin on 'What are we personally hoping for from this project?' or 'What are our departments hoping to get out of this working party?' Of course, there is no guarantee that people will be open about their motives. However, if you are prepared to be open about your agendas, particularly if you occupy a position of authority, others are more likely to be open about theirs – and then the group has far more of the information it needs to be effective. Resolving the differences may still be difficult, but at least everyone knows where everyone stands and the group is likely to waste less time reaching the performing stage.

The second type of imbalance in self-awareness – when other group members know things about an individual that the individual does not realise him or herself – is a **blind spot**. A typical example of a blind spot is a situation where the group is unwilling to tell someone that the real reason why her or his offer of help is not being accepted is because no one believes that she or he can do it.

One of the main reasons for blind spots is that the group members are afraid of hurting the feelings of another group member. It is never easy to tell people that you do not feel that they are competent, or that you do not trust them. However, while blind spots remain, the individual concerned is clearly disadvantaged. This individual can do nothing to challenge the assumptions of the rest of the group, or try to change his or her own behaviour. Again, the best remedy is usually to try sensitively to bring the situation out into the open. It may be better for a member of the group to tell the individual about the group's feelings in private, to reduce the chances of public humiliation and to give the person a chance to collect his or her thoughts before having to deal with the whole group.

As the examples described here show, both hidden agendas and blind spots can damage the effectiveness of groups. Increasing a group's level of openness and 'self-awareness' of these problems can increase trust and release energy.

Group anxiety
Group relationships are on the whole more stressful than individual relationships, and generally the larger the group, the greater the stress. People tend to feel exposed, on show, uncertain of where they fit in. This is particularly true in new groups and at large formal gatherings and meetings. There is less opportunity for immediate confirmation and feedback from other people and more space for fantasies to grow about what other people think or intend.

The anxiety this causes can be coped with creatively or destructively, both collectively by the group and by individuals. Collectively, the group may develop norms and structures that will alleviate anxiety and create a good working environment. Individually, people may develop communication skills and personal sensitivity that will reduce the element of fantasy in the group and promote personal contact. Alternatively, individuals may be left to cope in their own characteristic and idiosyncratic ways with whatever anxiety they feel. People may:

- talk too much through embarrassment
- intellectualise to get away from the anxious feelings
- chat to a neighbour to get some personal contact
- be so worried that they cannot listen and then ask irrelevant questions
- turn up late because they are worried about coming at all, or as a form of silent protest
- make bad jokes at inopportune moments
- attack and criticise others because they are afraid of being attacked themselves
- stray from the point because they are too anxious to concentrate
- smooth over all difficulties, try to keep things 'nice' and avoid confrontation
- continually apologise for themselves.

More seriously, people may:

- withdraw, hide, try to become inconspicuous
- look for someone stronger to protect them or ally themselves with the person most likely to win, regardless of the ally's views
- look for someone to attack and begin hostilities against the nearest likely victim – this often leads to scapegoating (the situation where one person, often a 'weaker' member of the group or its leader, is unreasonably and unfairly blamed for a group's difficulties), where the group fantasises that, if this person is excluded, all its problems will disappear.

It is common for people to feel anxious about:

- belonging and fitting in
- their value to the group
- how criticism and conflict will be dealt with.

One of the very important maintenance functions of a group, discussed earlier, is to ensure that these sources of group anxiety are dealt with in a way that is felt to be constructive and mutually acceptable.

Groupthink

Groupthink is a term that was coined by Irving Janis, who was intrigued by how teams arrive at devastating decisions by ignoring evidence that might suggest that what they are planning to do or have done is ill-advised (Janis, 1972). By far some of the most famous cases include decisions to take military action when circumstances make a successful outcome highly unlikely, for example, the 'Bay of Pigs' attempted invasion of Cuba in 1961. More recent suggested examples include the 1986 *Challenger* space shuttle disaster (Esser and Lindoerfer, 1989, pp. 167–77) and the 2006 *Nimrod* disaster (Sengupta, 2009). In each case warnings were sounded about the dangers, but these were ignored. Janis suggests that under certain conditions commitment to the group overrides ability to assess situations realistically. These conditions are:

1   The group faces a situation where an important decision has to be made, under severe time pressure.

2   The group is already fairly cohesive.

3   The group has a tendency to isolate itself from outsiders.

4   The leader has a preferred solution, which the group actively pursues.

It is important for groups, especially ones that are close-knit, to realise that they are liable to groupthink, which can be recognised by the following symptoms:

• an exaggerated sense of the group's importance and a feeling of invulnerability

• unanimity

• the rationalising away of less-preferred options

• appeals to morality

• stereotyping of opponents in negative terms

• pressure on members to conform

• self-censorship of doubts.

There are several possible defences against groupthink. First, try to ensure that important groups contain people with some diversity of opinions. Second, try to aim for a moderate, rather than a high degree of consensus in the group. If there is a high degree of consensus, then invite one or two people to play the role of devil's advocate, taking up contrary views for the sake of argument. Alternatively, new members with different ideas could be invited into the group – the disadvantage here being that the group would need to reform, which, of course, takes time.

Both groupthink and **scapegoating** are often processes by which groups resist making changes to the group and how it works. Groups resist changes for many of the reasons that individuals do – they have their own vested interests to protect and to admit that they are wrong may cause members pain and discomfort.

Stop and reflect

Are there ways in which teams you have been involved in have become dysfunctional? What was done about this if anything?

Dealing with conflict

Conflict is inevitable in any organisation and effective management involves managing differences, disagreement and conflict. However, there are four brief points to consider:

• Many of the conflicts that you have to deal with in organisations are not as awful as you might fear. The anticipation of what might happen is often far worse than the more humdrum reality. Very often, people want to work things out to make working life reasonable.

• Quite a lot of conflict is organisational. It is the position you represent, or the department or organisation, that is in conflict, rather than you as an individual.

2: Working with people

- An external support network can be valuable. As well as support and reassurance, it could offer you a relatively impartial view of issues that you may not be able to view dispassionately.

- Conflict can be constructive. Without different perspectives, there would be little creative development.

The 'layers' in organisational conflict

A useful way of categorising the causes of conflict is to think of these differences and the resulting disagreements as comprising various interrelated layers. Conflict will often involve several of these layers. As a result, quite different sorts of disagreements and sources of conflict are superimposed on each other, making the conflict difficult to analyse and pin down. It is worth distinguishing five different layers as follows.

Misunderstandings

These are differences and conflicts resulting from genuine misconceptions about what is said or implied – people 'getting hold of the wrong end of the stick'.

Differences in values and beliefs

People's values and beliefs influence how they view and act on the world. Differences in values are likely to manifest themselves in disagreements over how the organisation should be run. For example, people may disagree over whether to accept sponsorship or assistance from particular companies.

Differences in interest

These arise primarily from competition for scarce 'goods' and resources. These 'goods' may be things that people want as individuals: status, power and position, or the difference can arise as departments or sections compete for limited resources in the organisation.

Interpersonal differences

For all kinds of reasons, people can have difficulty in 'getting on' with others – differences in personality, temperament or style may be involved. A 'personality clash' is the usual term for it.

Feelings and emotions

It is difficult to separate hurt feelings from the content of that with which we disagree. Equally, conflict itself can arouse strong emotions and lead to further conflict. Emotions aroused in one situation can easily spill over into another situation, and often we only realise after the turbulent meeting that it was what we represented there that was attacked, rather than us personally.

If we consider these layers, then it seems clear that misunderstandings can often be sorted out fairly easily once they have been recognised. However, misunderstandings may reflect 'deeper' differences and conflicts, which are usually more difficult to resolve. They may also be symptoms of wider problems of communication or structural issues in the organisation.

Differences in values and beliefs give rise to the everyday conflicts over the 'what should we do?' and 'how shall we do it?' issues in organisations. For example, arguments over whether to develop business in certain parts of the world where there is conflict and international condemnation.

Differences in interest can give rise to quite bitter conflict. Often because these differences are 'spiced' with values and beliefs, we tend to believe the interests for which we are fighting are 'right'.

Interpersonal differences and feelings and emotions are unlikely to occur in a 'pure' form; other layers of conflict will usually be present as well.

Recognising conflict
Before you can begin to deal with conflict, you need to be able to recognise that it exists. In many cases the signs of conflict will be all too obvious and visible – there may be arguments, 'sniping', rows, raised tempers and emotions, possibly even formal disputes and grievances.

Such conflicts are easy to spot, but many conflicts are much less visible. Like an iceberg, they lie mainly submerged below the surface of everyday life in the organisation. However, as with icebergs, there is usually something visible above the surface if you look carefully. Some signs of potential hidden conflict include:

- a coolness or rigid formality in relations between the individuals or groups involved
- difficult or uncomfortable silences at meetings
- issues that seem to keep coming back on the agenda of meetings time after time but never seem to be resolved
- an unwillingness to communicate between individuals or groups
- one individual or group 'putting down' another
- the withdrawal of parties from discussions and the avoidance of certain issues
- constant referral to formal rules and procedures.

The list of symptoms looks deceptively simple, but what you may actually experience could be some partial showing of some symptoms, or some combination of the above.

Conflict is not necessarily bad or unproductive, either from the point of view of the organisation as a whole or from the point of view of the individuals or groups within it. Indeed, Tuckman's group development process suggests that some conflict is likely and necessary for growth to occur. It is important to realise that whether a conflict is viewed as constructive or destructive will depend very much on the position and point of view of the people observing it. A dispute between two departmental managers over their respective share of new resources may benefit the organisation because it creates a better understanding of the two departments' needs, but it may be painful for one or both of the individuals involved.

Evaluating the situation

Before deciding what strategy to use to try to resolve conflict, it is wise to evaluate the situation. You will need to consider factors such as the seriousness of the conflict, the timescale – whether it needs to be resolved quickly or whether a more leisurely response is acceptable – whether it is a win–lose or a win–win conflict, and your own power, personal preferences and strengths and weaknesses in dealing with conflict. If the conflict is relatively trivial or just a 'healthy' disagreement, you may decide that it is better to let it run its course without involvement. However, if there is a danger of the conflict escalating and becoming destructive, you will want to intervene. What follows, then, is an examination of the various strategies you might adopt, the situations in which they will be appropriate and their likely effectiveness.

Choosing appropriate strategies – the five principal approaches

The different strategies to use in response to conflict can be grouped into five broad approaches.

1   *Ignoring*

    The uncertainty and varied emotions that are frequently involved in conflict can lead to uncomfortable feelings of anxiety or threat. One way of trying to escape these difficulties is to ignore the problem. In many cases this may not matter – the conflict may not be very deep or it may be a result of healthy differences of opinion. However, the danger is that the conflict may be destructive, in which case your failure to deal with it may be seen as an avoidance of your managerial responsibilities.

2   *Allowing*

    If the conflict is constructive, or likely to be temporary or relatively trivial, then you might deliberately allow it to run its course. If emotions are aroused or if people's feelings are hurt and they are upset, you might want to take some action to help smooth the situation. This may involve giving individuals support, allowing them to explain their feelings and encouraging them to put the conflict in perspective. Alternatively, if you are not sure how the conflict will develop, you may prefer to adopt a watching brief, allowing the conflict to happen but keeping an eye on it in case it becomes destructive and you need to intervene.

3   *Reducing or containing*

    Strategies aimed at reducing or containing the conflict can be further divided into short-term, 'quick fix' responses and medium-term responses that will probably be more effective in the long term. Short-term strategies would include persuasion, coercion, arbitration and buying-off. Medium-term strategies include separating the parties, mediation, appeals and confrontation.

4   *Resolving*

    Resolving strategies aim to find a longer-term resolution to the conflict. They not only try to deal with the present problem, but also create the conditions where destructive conflict is less likely to occur in future. This may be done by establishing common goals, organisational restructuring, improving communication and integrative bargaining.

5 *Preventing*

Probably the most effective way of dealing with destructive conflict is to try to prevent it happening in the first place. Given that people and groups will always have differences, and sometimes irreconcilable ones, how can you achieve this? The answer is that you cannot achieve it with certainty but that your best chance will lie in encouraging a climate in which people seek win–win solutions rather than win–lose solutions.

Conclusion to Chapter 2

You should now be more familiar both with theories and concepts concerning how people are motivated (or demotivated!) and with ideas and issues concerning how people work in teams and groups. You should see that engagement with the issues of motivation and team-working are complex and require much thought and sensitivity to both individual preferences and what is good for the team, group or organisation as a whole. You should also be able to summarise the main ideas of each theory or concept in your own words, offering suitable examples as illustrations of the particular factors or relationships involved.

The first section of this chapter looked in some depth at the concept of motivation, examining many of the main theories. In content theories, the works of Maslow, Alderfer, McGregor and Herzberg were considered, while in process theories expectancy, equity and goal-setting theory were considered. Content theories attempt to identify individual needs or motives and suggest how each activates different behaviours. Maslow, for example, identified five hierarchical levels of needs: physiological, security, social, esteem and self-actualisation. Alderfer then took Maslow's theory and collapsed the five hierarchical levels into three types of need: existence, relatedness and growth. McGregor suggested that assumptions associated with Theory X management were easily found in the workplace and that this explained how workers behaved in a particular way in response to the way in which management conducted themselves. Herzberg focused on work motivation and claimed that employers who simply provided what he termed hygiene factors would not motivate their staff. Instead he thought managers should focus on making the work itself more interesting.

Process theories were examined next. Equity theory suggests that motivation is moderated by the perceived fairness or discrepancy between personal contributions and rewards relative to what others receive. Expectancy theory provides the central explanation of motivation as a process. It suggests how individuals evaluate effort–performance–outcome relationships in making behaviour choices. Goal-setting theory goes one step further in attempting to link motivation directly to job performance.

However, all these theories of motivation that were examined and discussed tend to focus on the employee as an individual. Some cultures, in contrast, emphasise not the individual but the group (family, tribe, village or team) as the centre of attention. The challenge for you as a manager is to determine how, when you go into a different cultural context, you balance individuals and/or groups in terms of motivation.

This leads on to the second section of this chapter, the focus of which was the complex issue of team- and group working. Many managers focus on task rather than people in their desire to get things done (Blake and Mouton, 1964), but in the case of team development, this can have a negative, counter-productive effect. The ideas presented in this section were intended to help you think through the issues involved in developing effective teams – particularly those that can function at a distance and using new technologies. But in reality, much effective team-working in whatever context stems from careful thinking on the part of the manager about group processes. Managers must pay attention to the needs of both the organisation and the individual group members – a goal that applies not only to team-working but also to motivation and all aspects of working with people.

3: Managing people

Introduction

In this chapter you will be introduced to **human resource management (HRM)**. This is not simply because the effective management of people is central to organisational performance, but also because the rise of HRM reflects fundamental changes in contemporary organisations. As you will no doubt have experienced, the **employment relationship** (the legal link between employers and employees) has changed radically in the last ten to twenty years. Organisations face an increasingly competitive global environment and have been forced to respond in a number of ways. Many of these responses can be summarised by the four Ds of decentralisation, disaggregation, de-layering and disorganisation and as such have produced new patterns of employment and management practices that increasingly shape our working lives. Anyone working in a medium to large organisation in the last decade will have experienced a stream of organisational change programmes, from **total quality management (TQM)** to business process re-engineering, and from culture change to the **learning organisation**. At the same time, the composition of the staff in many organisations has been transformed. More recently, organisations have become more likely to include higher numbers of female staff, part-time workers and/or those on temporary contracts and working away from the workplace. This is because the key to organisational survival has been greater 'flexibility' in order to cut costs, retain a competitive advantage and access the skills needed by the organisation.

Decentralisation, disaggregation, de-layering and disorganisation are discussed later in this chapter.

It is in this context that HRM has become the major influence on contemporary employment management. This is not only because new forms of organisation and employment demand new ways of managing people, but that the logic of human resource management is precisely to instigate and shape such changes. Therefore, the first section of this chapter will outline the key elements of HRM as a distinctive approach to employment relations and will examine the sometimes competing views that have emerged regarding its key principles. The following sections will consider how these principles are realised in three key areas of the human resource function. These are organisational entry, performance management and training and development. One of the central tenets of HRM is that it offers an integrated approach to people management. In this respect, these three functional areas should be seen as integral and interrelated elements in achieving and maintaining a human resource strategy.

3.1: The development of HRM

It is not unusual for managers starting MBAs to admit that they lack knowledge of disciplines such as accounting or marketing but they tend to think that they know what personnel or HRM entails. It is frequently seen as the responsibility of a designated group of people within the organisation – the personnel department – concerning the administrative aspects of employing people and maintaining harmonious, productive relationships.

These aspects might include recruitment, maintaining pay and conditions, and running training courses. Perhaps because personnel management has been considered to be relatively mundane, it has often been held in low esteem in many Western businesses, while finance and marketing have been seen as more specialist and thus more important.

However, an expanded understanding of the issues raised by – and the skills required for – effective people management has gone hand in hand with a growing recognition of the importance of people in the organisation (Berger and Berger, 2004). This is not to say that, in practice, good managers have not always recognised the importance of people management, but demographic trends, new technologies and growing demand for skilled workers – as well as innovation in management practices – are combining to give the art of managing people a more formal, high-profile place at the centre of the organisation's priorities.

One result of this reappraisal of the role of people management in organisations is a shift towards replacing 'personnel management' with a more widely encompassing 'human resource management' (Marchington and Wilkinson, 2006). HRM is usually thought of as being less functionally based than personnel management, and it implies a greater role for managers throughout the organisation in managing people. So, as well as an expansion in the content of people management, the set of people who are tasked with discharging these duties is changing, but the major problems of employing people in organisations remain, because they are rooted in the human condition itself (Tyson and York, 1996, p. 3). Suddenly, managing people seems far less straightforward than at first sight.

Accordingly there has been an important debate in the management literature about whether a set of practices known as 'human resource management' is replacing more traditional personnel management. The key features of this debate structure many of the assumptions that underpin much current managerial thinking and practice. One of the principal subjects of debate is the question of what constitutes HRM and how it differs from personnel management. Answers to this question can be summarised as:

- HRM represents a set of policies and practices for managing people that are integrated with the wider strategy of the business.
- HRM describes a set of policies toward employees notable for its internal consistency.
- HRM represents the acceptance by the organisation that its strategy should be based on the capabilities of its human resources.
- HRM gives line managers a wider set of responsibilities for policies concerning managing people and leads to a less prominent role for personnel specialists.
- HRM captures the view that people are the prime resource of the organisation.

There is much debate about HRM, its nature, meanings and effects, which has resulted in some aspects of HRM being perceived as controversial. You should also be aware that these debates are essential to understanding its differing aspects. For example, some of these definitions may be contradictory – proponents of the first view, that HRM entails an integration of strategy with approaches to managing people, often look for representation of the personnel function on the main board as an indication that HRM is being practised. The very opposite could be true under the fourth definition, however, which requires a much more diffuse means of discharging HRM functions.

Indeed, the question of how human resource functions are discharged is intimately bound up with deciding what policies to pursue, so the issue has great practical as well as academic importance. On this point, the writer David Guest has no doubts: 'if human resource management is to be taken seriously, personnel managers must give it away … Paradoxically, therefore, giving it away seems to result in personnel management issues becoming more important' (1987, p. 510). This means that all managers have some responsibility for doing HRM.

HRM versus personnel management

John Storey has set out a model of what he regards as the essential elements of HRM, which he defines as 'a distinctive approach to employment management which seeks to achieve competitive advantage through the strategic deployment of a highly committed and capable workforce, using an integrated array of cultural, structural and personnel techniques' (1995, p. 5). These elements are as outlined below.

1 Beliefs and assumptions
- That it is the human resource that gives competitive edge.
- That the aim should not be mere compliance with rules, but employee commitment.
- That employees should be very carefully selected and developed.

2 Strategic qualities
- Because of the above factors, HRM decisions are of strategic importance.
- Top management involvement is necessary.
- HRM policies should be integrated into the business strategy – stemming from it and even contributing to it.

3 Critical role of managers
- Because HRM practice is critical to the core activities of the business, it is too important to be left to personnel specialists alone.
- Line managers need to be closely involved both as deliverers and drivers of the HRM policies.
- Much greater attention should be paid to the management of managers themselves.

> 4   Key levels
>
> ○   Managing culture is more important than managing procedures and systems.
>
> ○   Integrated action on selection, communication, training, reward and development.
>
> ○   Restructuring and job redesign to allow devolved responsibility and empowerment.
>
> (Source: Storey, 1995, p. 7)

There are particular elements of this definition and model that you should recognise. First, HRM is described as a 'distinctive approach'. This means that it is seen as representing a fundamental shift from previous practices to employment management.

Second, you should appreciate the emphasis on the 'strategic role' of HRM. This means that there is a belief that the human resource offers potential for competitive advantage, and thus, HRM should be an integral part of the process of setting the strategy of the organisation, with board and line management involvement rather than a restricted functional area (this point is discussed further below).

Third, HRM policies should be integrated. This means that respective elements of the function should be internally consistent and designed to meet wider strategic goals.

Finally, HRM is said to differ from 'traditional personnel management' through its greater emphasis on developing *a highly committed* workforce. In the past, personnel management largely located itself as 'between' management and workers and was therefore predominately occupied with regulating their agreements or facilitating resolution when they broke down. Now, however, HRM is seen as central to the creation of commitment in staff.

 Stop and reflect

What is your experience of the personnel function in your working life? Does this experience match the expectations of the HRM model?

Models of HRM

It must also be recognised that some view HRM as simply a re-labelling of existing practice. This view suggests that although many personnel managers have had their titles changed, their essential activities remain unchanged. Consequently, there is some scepticism regarding the claims of HRM to transform the employment relationship, particularly when there is an obvious gap between its theoretical claims and its practical implementation.

Even where it is believed that substantive change has occurred, there are differences in understanding about the nature and philosophy of this change.

For example, one view sees HRM as representing an extension of management control over those aspects of the employment relationship that were previously regarded as jointly agreed between employees and managers. Employees are in this view now seen as solely the responsibility of management. An alternative perspective weakens some of these assertions and presents HRM as an individually focused development model. This development model of HRM treats the individual as a resource rather than an expense. It follows that expenditure on, for example, training should also be seen as an investment and not an expense. This view suggests that organisation and personal development are interlinked and that HRM has an obligation to maximise the potential of employees. These two models of HRM have been called '**hard**' and '**soft**' respectively.

Hard HRM emphasises the quantitative, calculative and business strategy aspects of managing the human resource in a rational fashion. In this sense, employees are to be treated as any other economic factor. This is the traditional market-led approach under which managers seek to control employees, subject to an overall business strategy.

The 'soft' variant is a developmental model that has its roots in the human relations school and emphasises the importance of people issues such as communication, motivation, leadership, training and development. Rather than control and compliance, it seeks mutual commitment to wider organisational goals.

It is important, therefore, that you appreciate the different perspectives that inform HRM. You need to recognise that it is precisely because there are different perspectives that an extremely vigorous debate on the nature of the employment relationship in contemporary organisations has been stimulated. You should recognise that there are different models of HRM, all of which have slightly different underlying assumptions.

HRM and organisational flexibility

The rise of HRM has also been linked to wider developments in how organisations work in the twenty-first century, particularly in Western nations. These can be summarised by the four Ds of decentralisation, disaggregation, de-layering and disorganisation (Thompson and McHugh, 2002). These ideas, summarised in turn below, propose broad trends, and organisational realities are often more complex than can be captured in these models. Change may, in most cases, be more piecemeal than outlined here.

Decentralisation

Organisations are said to be decentralising when they divide their large bureaucratic structures into smaller and more independent units, operating as autonomous profit centres with delegated decision-making powers. The integration between these autonomous units is supposedly secured through the overall organisational strategy, information systems and culture. Thus, they are (hypothetically) guided by a 'shared vision' rather than by rules, memos and managerial control.

Disaggregation

This goes beyond the internal restructuring of organisations and refers to the break-up of large organisations into networks of small firms. Organisations are reduced to an essential core and then sub-contract non-core activities to smaller companies.

De-layering

This refers to a shift towards flatter, less hierarchical forms of organisation where whole layers of middle management are removed, and vertical lines of communication and authority are replaced by horizontal communication between self-managing teams.

Disorganisation

The idea contained in the term 'disorganisation' is that bureaucratic structures and rational planning processes are no longer appropriate in a supposedly increasingly turbulent and unpredictable environment.

Taken together, the four trends outlined above point to radically new and, perhaps, more empowering forms of working in organisations. However, it is important to realise that not everyone sees these trends as positive. Critics have pointed out that not everyone benefits from these changes. In fact, for those who do not benefit, work has become more insecure and disempowering.

Another way of looking at these tendencies is through Atkinson's influential notion of the 'flexible firm' (1984). For Atkinson, the flexible firm has replaced predictable homogeneous employment patterns, standardised contracts and uniform payment systems with more varied and flexible working arrangements. These allow a closer match to be achieved between the type and amount of labour available, and the nature and volume of work demands. Consequently, the flexible firm is made up of two groups of employees:

- a 'core' of highly trained workers on full-time, permanent contracts, who tend to possess key skills and, as a result, enjoy high status, job security and good career prospects
- a 'periphery' of temporary, part-time, casual and mainly low-skilled workers (although the periphery also includes 'knowledge workers' selling their skills on a freelance basis) on 'non-standard' employment contracts.

Atkinson suggests that flexibility can take four different forms:

Functional flexibility: this refers to the ability of firms to reorganise jobs, so that the jobholder can deploy her/his skills across a broader range of tasks. It enables the organisation to make more effective use of permanent full-time staff by re-deploying them across various jobs and parts of the organisation according to needs.

Numerical flexibility: this denotes the ability of the organisation to adjust the number of workers, or the level of hours worked in line with changes in demand for them. Numerical flexibility can take different forms and includes part-time work, temporary work, reduction of employment security for full-time staff and modification of working time patterns to reflect patterns of work pressure (e.g. overtime, shift working, annual hours contract).

Distancing (or sub-contracting): this refers to the displacement of employment contracts by commercial contracts whereby a company may simply contract out peaks in workload to another individual or organisation.

Financial flexibility: this refers to the move away from single payment systems, towards variable and individualised payment systems, seeking a closer relationship between individual contributions and reward (e.g. performance related pay, profit-sharing).

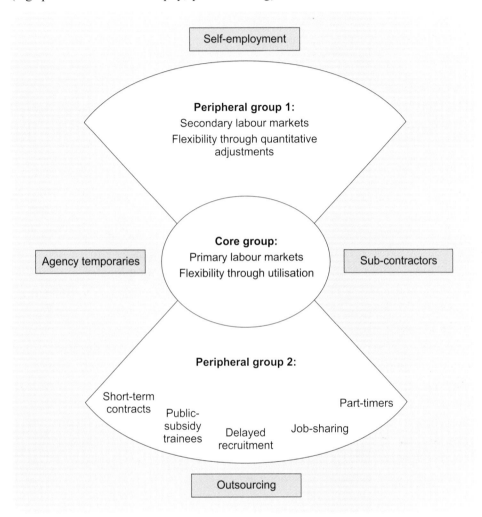

Figure 3.1: The flexible firm model

However, researchers such as Legge (2005) have highlighted many points of contradiction between the concept of flexibility and the rhetoric of HRM. First, while flexibility is one of the core values of HRM, there are some significant tensions between certain forms of flexibility (in particular, numerical flexibility) and other HRM values, such as quality and commitment. The pursuit of numerical flexibility via temporary working is unlikely to produce commitment and quality. Second, there is a tension between numerical and functional flexibility. Functional flexibility is dependent on a satisfactory degree of employment security, stability and commitment, which are all likely to be eroded by the introduction of numerical flexibility. So jobs that are subject to numerical flexibility are unlikely to be done by core workers. Firms are less willing to train periphery workers to be more flexible in their work skills, and these workers have little motive to supply functional flexibility.

Consequently, there are somewhat opposing views on the effects of flexibility. Positive views (e.g. Garsten, 1999; Bone, 2006) have tended to celebrate flexibility as holding the promise of increased worker empowerment and participation at work. In this view, labour market flexibility offers individuals new freedom in controlling their working lives and in balancing home and work. Here it is argued that while job security and predictable careers have been lost, this is not something to lament since flexibility affords new possibilities for inter-organisational, inter-occupational moves, and for combining work, family and leisure. This is certainly the case for some workers, especially those with high skills that are in short supply.

However, there is also a negative view of organisational flexibility. Here flexibility is associated with a movement towards increasing cost cutting, the casualisation of labour and work intensification within labour markets. Numerical flexibility is often associated with casualisation rather than empowerment or better work–life balance (Thompson and McHugh, 2002). Moreover, as Surman (2002) outlines, although the liberty promised by flexible working practices such as teleworking enabled by modern technologies has been widely celebrated (e.g. DTI, 2002), the uncertainties produced by 'flexible' working arrangements have the potential to create anxiety. Workers must find new ways of managing what they often perceive as an irregular working arrangement. Without the geographical distinction between home and work, Surman found that workers often lost a division that had informed and organised their social practices. Far from inducing a more liberating work–life balance, flexible working practices like teleworking actually brought into question a worker's everyday activities and were something that they found both unsettling and disconcerting. Workers now had to make their own decisions about how, when and where to work, decisions that had previously been made for them. While on the one hand this allowed greater freedom, it also created new pressures. Inevitably, the way workers chose to organise their work had implications for family life. For example, children had to be instructed that while their parents were at home they were actually 'at work'.

Lastly, while various forms of numerical flexibility were once reserved to cover for special periods, they are increasingly being used as a managerial strategy to keep costs down and pass on risk (Lambert, 2008). Recent studies have also shown that programmes of work re-organisation designed to increase functional flexibility may only result in limited autonomy for workers; this is the case, for example, when the existing hierarchy remains unchanged and constrains the amount of responsibility and power that is delegated to lower levels (Thompson and McHugh, 2002). It should also be recognised that traditional mass production based on cheap and semi-skilled labour is still widespread. For example, Ngai and Smith (2007) in their study of manufacturing plants in China suggest that such practices, which to some extent have disappeared from industrialised economies in Europe and North America, have merely been relocated to developing countries.

International HRM

The previous point about traditional mass production moving to developing nations is an example of the international dimension of HRM. International HRM has been defined by Scullion as 'the human resource management issues and problems arising from the internationalisation of business, and the human resource strategies, policies and practices which firms pursue in response to the internationalisation process' (1995, p. 354). It is important to acknowledge that there is a distinction between considering HRM from a 'comparative' and considering it from an 'international' perspective and that these emerge from distinct theoretical traditions that ask different questions about the nature of HRM.

The *comparative* approach is concerned with understanding *why* HRM practices differ across different countries. This orientation considers the different institutional and cultural structures associated with a nation that have an impact on the human relations approaches of employing organisations. These include legal and regulatory frameworks, systems of industrial relations and employment practices. The emphasis on these differences encourages us to consider to what extent human resource policies adopted in one country might be applicable elsewhere or whether they need to be adapted to meet particular national contexts.

In contrast, the *international* perspective is concerned with the practices of multinational organisations that have operations in different countries. This perspective considers the methods necessary to manage these organisations' internationally diverse and geographically dispersed workforces in order to secure both global and local competitive advantages. These methods include global management succession planning, selection and training for the expatriate experience and management of the local labour market. In contrast to the comparative approach, 'international' HRM is prescriptive in its orientation and tends towards proposing universal approaches to 'international' problems. The comparative differences between national contexts are largely ignored in favour of 'global' practices that are implemented throughout an organisation's territories.

A common debate in the international HRM literature is that between '**convergence and divergence**' approaches to understanding the development of human resource practices. The convergence thesis argues that the process of globalisation and development of international trade will lead, in time, to a convergence of national business environments, including human resource approaches, as developing economies industrialise. In other words, industrialisation creates similar patterns of management and organisation irrespective of national context. However, evidence for this is mixed (Rowley and Bae, 2002; Jacoby, 2005). Within Europe and the Asia-

Pacific region there remain significant differences in business practices despite economies being well advanced. National, regional and local cultures continue to influence approaches to employment management. Consequently, the idea that the 'best' HR practices have 'universal' application lacks empirical support. At best, it is argued that globalisation might be causing some degree of limited convergence across regional clusters such as China, South Korea and Japan (Rowley et al., 2004). However, even within these clusters significant differences remain.

Having established in this introduction the principles and philosophy underpinning HRM as a distinctive approach to employment management, in the following sections we will examine how these principles are realised in three key areas of the HR function. These are organisational entry, managing performance and rewards, and training and development.

3.2: Organisational entry

This section considers the key steps in the organisational entry process and:

- examines the process of organisational entry
- reviews alternative methods that can be used to design and control organisational entry
- considers the importance of induction for successful organisational entry
- recognises that organisational entry is also a process that must be managed.

The success of an organisation depends on people who work for it. Hiring the 'right' person for the job, developing the potential of those with promise and holding on to those with outstanding or unusual ability have always been important concerns of organisations. Recruitment and selection decisions are among the most important decisions that managers make on behalf of their organisations. Consider the financial ramifications of recruiting someone. Imagine that you recruit someone on a short-term contract at an average salary of €30,000 per annum for three years. In salary alone, this is a €90,000 decision. On top of this, there are the employer's state employment taxes, training and retraining costs, and office overheads, which are often estimated to double the cost of employing someone.

However, as you saw in the previous section, effective selection is even more important under HRM since it sees people as being the key to competitive advantage. The integration of HRM with strategy has led to the use of practices that link the selection decisions (e.g. the profile of ideal candidates) with the overall competitive strategy of the organisation. Therefore, it is not only the costs of employing someone that make recruitment and selection decisions important. In this section, you will be introduced to the process of organisational entry and will consider the different choices that have to be made concerning the adoption of appropriate methods of selection and induction.

The process of organisational entry

Efforts to find new members of staff often concentrate on either recruitment (the attraction of a pool of candidates) or selection (choosing between applicants). Recruitment and selection are commonly seen as discrete tasks that can be carried out with little regard to each other. In practice, though, these two processes interact not only with each other but also with other processes, such as job analysis and induction. This interaction can be displayed as a process model (Figure 3.2) that illustrates the sequence of events common to organisational entry programmes.

By 'analysis' we refer to the whole set of activities through which the organisation determines its human resource requirements. This should involve, at the strategic level, deciding what jobs are needed, an analysis of each vacant job to decide if it needs filling or redesigning, and determining the characteristics required of individuals to fill it effectively. 'Recruitment' is geared to attracting or finding a pool of candidates with the required characteristics. 'Selection' involves choosing the most suitable candidate from within that resulting pool – many and various methods exist to do this, such as interviews, psychometric tests and work simulation exercises. 'Induction', the final step in the process, refers to the activities that help smooth the transition for a new appointee from outsider to member of the organisation – a process that is important both for the productivity of the organisation and for the mental wellbeing of the employee.

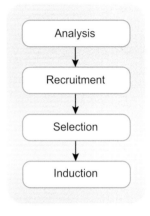

Figure 3.2:
Organisational entry: a process model

Despite the importance of the organisational entry process, both for the organisation and for those involved in the process, most managers have little training either in the issues underlying the process or in the best practice of selection and recruitment. Here we introduce some theoretical perspectives to help structure your thinking about organisational entry.

Different approaches to organisational entry

Approaches to organisational entry are underpinned by different assumptions about people and the factors that determine their behaviour at work. You need to be aware of these different assumptions in order to make informed choices about which methods suit particular circumstances. To illustrate this, the following three different approaches to organisational entry will be considered: person–job fit, social negotiation and person–organisation fit.

Person–job fit

The traditional approach to recruitment and selection is based on the view that organisations should specify as closely as possible the requirements of the job and then look for individuals whose personal attributes fit those requirements. Hence, this is often called the 'person–job fit' approach. It is founded on an assumption that human behaviour is determined by factors internal to the individual, for example their particular skills, aptitudes and attitudes, with the implication that selection techniques should be concerned with accessing and measuring these internal, personal factors, which can then be compared against those required for the job.

The person–job fit approach has been criticised for a variety of reasons. In particular, the amount and pace of change means that the jobs for which people are recruited soon change; organisations may be interested in future outcomes such as promotability, as well as performance in a particular job; people influence the organisation's performance beyond the boundaries of their own jobs; and applicants also make decisions that affect the outcome of the entry process.

Social negotiation

The psychologist Peter Herriot (1992, 1993) has proposed an alternative organisational entry **paradigm**, which he terms the 'social negotiation' approach. The following ideas are central to this approach:

- that people are constantly changing
- that people's self-perceptions are important
- that jobs are constantly changing
- that the selection that takes place is of both parties by each other
- that information is exchanged
- that negotiation takes place
- that the purpose of the process is to establish a **psychological contract**, or to discover that one is not feasible.

The proposed outcome of the social negotiation approach is the psychological contract. This term is used to denote the unwritten expectations about what employees anticipate from employers in terms of compensation and how they will be developed and also employer's expectations about the loyalty and diligence of the people who work for them.

Importantly, the social negotiation approach highlights that both parties – applicant and organisation – make decisions about whether to continue in the organisational entry process. In this approach, the goal of organisational entry is to help the newcomer perform better by enhancing their understanding and motivation during the process. This is in contrast to the person–job fit approach, which aims only to identify the person who will perform best in the particular job.

It is important to recognise that these two approaches are built on fundamentally different assumptions about the determinants of people's behaviour. The person–job fit approach assumes that the factors that determine people's behaviour come from within the individual – that people have personality traits that are consistent and endure. The social negotiation approach, on the other hand, is based on the idea that factors external to the individual have an important bearing on the individual's behaviour.

Person–organisation fit

This perspective emphasises that human behaviour stems from an interaction of person and situation, of internal and external characteristics. This is important for organisational entry for four reasons:

1 It suggests that if an organisation wants to predict an applicant's behaviour and their performance, the organisation needs to analyse the applicant's 'fit' with the organisation's culture.

2 It emphasises the importance of creating an environment that suits newcomers, and of creating a job that is satisfying and motivates the individual.

3   It acknowledges that high performance in one situation does not necessarily mean that the person will perform well in a new situation. Therefore, this perspective prompts the manager to explore the reasons why a person has performed well in their existing situation – that is, how the person interacts with the situational factors in their current job – so that the manager can consider how the person will behave in a new situation.

4   That recruitment has a future dimension. Individuals may be expected to make future contributions to the organisation that lie outside the work role to which they are presently being recruited.

Thus, a potentially more flexible approach to recruitment and selection is to replace the traditional focus on the job with a more person-orientated approach (Iles and Salaman, 1995) which focuses on the generic qualities and behaviours required by the organisation. These more generic qualities have been referred to as competencies. The competency approach is based on the identification of behaviours, skills, knowledge and attributes that underline successful performance and differentiate excellent performers from poor ones. It provides a more flexible approach to selection than a job-orientated approach in that it can be used to identify characteristics that are relevant across the organisation and are related to organisational competitiveness. Thus competency frameworks are usually seen as being compatible with HRM initiatives such as flexibility, team-working and multi-skilling because they are not constrained by jobs but rather relate more broadly to the general qualities associated with competitiveness.

Bearing these different perspectives in mind, it is now possible to examine the different steps involved in the recruitment and selection process briefly, starting with activities designed to identify and attract suitable candidates and ending with a review of the different methods used to choose the 'best candidate'.

Stop and reflect

Consider an organisation like Microsoft or Google. Do you think it would make sense for these organisations to recruit the candidate that had the best technical expertise for the job but who did not fit the culture of the organisation? What would be the consequences of this recruitment decision?

The organisational entry process

Analysis

Short-term job analysis
Organisational entry often starts with traditional methods of job analysis. The organisation asks 'What do we require to accomplish the current business of the organisation?' Short-term analysis requires the organisation to assess where it stands with regard to the:

- tasks that must be completed
- skills required to do the work

- roles that need to be filled.

The idea is to gain a full understanding of the job, the qualities required to perform it effectively and the wider context of the job. This information is then written up as a job description that can be used to help future jobholders understand what is required of them. The job description is used, along with other information gathered during entry analysis, to produce a set of selection criteria. These criteria are the knowledge, skills, abilities and other attributes that jobholders must possess to be able to perform the job effectively. Selection criteria fall into two categories: essential criteria, which a person must be able to fulfil to be able to do the job – for example, a Heavy Goods Vehicle (HGV) licence for a lorry driver – and desirable criteria, which a person should be able to fulfil – for example, experience of driving a lorry in other countries. The selection criteria are the key factors that are used to decide who to recruit.

There are many job analysis tools that can be used when the organisation has to find someone for an existing job. The most common tools are observation, interviews (with anyone the jobholder will come into contact with, in addition to the current jobholder and the line manager), diaries, critical incident analysis, repertory grids, job inventories and work profiling. When a new job is created, managerial judgement is required to construct a complete job design.

Analysis of long-term objectives
This means thinking about how the job might develop and what qualities will be needed for the individual to develop within the organisation.

This type of analysis can be done along four lines of questioning:

- How might the job develop and change?
- How adaptable, flexible and able to learn is the individual?
- What are the organisation's long-term mission and objectives?
- How will the job help the incumbent develop?

Analysis of the organisational environment
This involves analysing the organisational environment the newcomer will experience. The organisational environment includes the job that the newcomer will do; the sub-culture and work group they will join; the organisation's mission, objectives, values and dominant culture; the technologies that are used; and the external environment in which the organisation is located. The task of the selector is to assess the interaction of the applicant with factors in the environments in which the applicant has performed well, to enable a considered estimate of person and environment interactions in the new organisation.

The reality of job analysis
Given the importance of organisational entry decisions, one might think that organisations would go to great lengths to analyse jobs and the environments in which people work. However, as many **industrial tribunals** have revealed, often very little analysis is done. Many managers believe that they instinctively understand the jobs of the people who work for them. Consequently, they may interview applicants with little idea of the real

nature of the job, of the skills and abilities they are looking for, or of how they will determine who the best candidate is. From the standpoint of the rational manager, such practices appear unambiguously bad. However, it should be noted that some (for example, Mintzberg and Waters, 1985) argue that *emergent* rather than pre-planned policies may be adequate or even preferable. Emergent policies are those that develop out of histories of trial and error or that involve an instinctive response that subtly reflects the culture and tradition of the organisation.

The person specification

On the basis of the job analysis the next step is to draw a 'person specification'. This is a profile of the 'ideal' candidate – that is, a list of characteristics that are considered necessary to perform the job well. There are various frameworks that can be used at this stage. However, it is increasingly argued that the traditional approach to recruitment and selection is too job-centred, or 'task-oriented'. In particular, it is argued that the ways in which job analyses are conducted and, hence, person specifications are designed tend to rely too heavily on the past and do not pay much attention to the changing requirements of the job and the organisation. The different ways in which the profile of the 'ideal' or 'best' candidate can be drawn up must be considered. The profile could be defined in terms of fitting the organisational culture or job specific expertise, or in respect of the likelihood that the candidate will stay with the organisation.

Recruitment and selection

Recruitment is the process of attracting a pool of applicants. This can be done in-house by members of the organisation or it can be sub-contracted to third parties. Having attracted a pool of candidates for a position, the most suitable candidate must be identified. However, the method used will be affected by the perspective held on organisational entry. For example, managers who take a person–job fit view of the process (whether consciously or unconsciously) will use tests designed to expose certain key psychological traits thought to be related to the intended job. The tests might take a variety of forms and examine skills and abilities, but whatever form the tests take, the purpose is to measure a person's fit to the job. Selectors who prefer the person–organisation fit approach will seek means to gauge the extent to which the person's skills, values and attributes complement those of the organisation.

Selection techniques and tests can help to discriminate between candidates, although in practice the formal interview remains an almost universal part of the selection process. However, recent research has shown an increasing use of selection methods other than the traditional interview. Many organisations now regularly use some form of testing – ability, aptitude, numeracy, literacy, and so on – in their selection processes.

The dominant methods of selection used in contemporary organisations will be reviewed below, but keep in mind that all have distinct strengths and weaknesses that need to be considered when they are adopted.

Interviews

Interviews are now used in almost all organisational entry exercises for almost all jobs, despite the fact that some contemporary research has suggested they are virtually useless at predicting the performance of applicants. The problems of interviews have been well noted. For example:

- Impressions formed in the first five minutes greatly influence the selection but are based on very little information.

- Interviewers tend to look for reasons to reject rather than for reasons to accept interviewees, which suggests the 'least bad' applicant gets the job.

- 'Halo and horns' – the interviewer's perception of one good or one bad impression produces an assumption that contaminates their perception of other comments. The candidate is quickly perceived positively (gaining a halo) or negatively (given horns) on the basis of limited evidence.

- Appearance affects an interviewer's judgement, even if irrelevant to the job.

- It is difficult to assess specialised skills and abilities in an interview.

- 'Recency' effects – the interviewer's recent experiences in his or her work environment may disproportionately influence the decisions taken.

Almost all organisations in almost all circumstances use the interview at some stage in their selection process. Similarly, most applicants expect to be interviewed. Therefore, the suspicion is that many organisations do not actually make a deliberate decision to use an interview based on an assessment of its particular suitability for the post to be filled. Instead the interview is simply the 'default' selection method.

Two final points need to be made about the interview. First, during the interview applicants develop much of their impression of what it would be like to work in the organisation. Therefore, the manner of the interview plays a major role in shaping the psychological contract between individual and organisation. Second, the interview is the only technique that currently exists that can be used to assess the interaction of individuals and environments. If you adopt a systematic approach to the investigation of this interaction, perhaps using a structured or semi-structured interview, as good employment practice suggests, you can gain evidence that should lead you to make a more realistic decision about the interviewee's fit to the organisation. It has also been argued that the validity and reliability of interviews as a selection method can be improved by increasing the number of interviewers (sequential, panel interviews) and structuring the interviews around standardised questions, including hypothetical questions relating to situations encountered in the job (e.g. 'What would you do if …?') (Newell and Shackleton, 2001).

Psychometric tests

A test has validity if it does what it is supposed to do; that is, select the candidates most likely to perform well in the job and reject those least likely to perform well. Reliability refers to whether a selection method, if repeated, would produce the same results.

Psychometric tests are a product of the influence of psychology and the search for scientific objectivity in HRM. There are two main types of test: cognitive and personality tests. **Cognitive tests** assess attributes such as intelligence, special ability or numerical ability; they have been found to have a relatively high predictive validity meaning they are good at identifying such abilities. However, some have questioned the extent to which they add to the information that could be obtained from simply looking at academic qualifications.

Personality tests assess individuals against a theoretical model of underlying personality factors. Many personality tests are available, with different levels of predictive validity. The use of psychometric tests has increased recently; however, this resurgent popularity raises questions about the ways in which they are used and manipulated by both organisations and candidates (e.g. Henderson et al., 1994; Newell and Shackleton, 2001). There are mixed feelings generally about testing – while tests are often defended on the basis of greater objectivity, the validity of some can be and has been called into question. Qualified psychologists are needed to interpret the results of the most sophisticated psychometrics and their relevance to the job and organisation.

Other selection techniques

There are many other selection techniques that can be used. Table 3.1 summarises the strengths and weaknesses of the main types of selection techniques.

Table 3.1: Summary of the main types of selection techniques

Selection technique	Description	Strengths	Weaknesses
Physical ability tests	Tests that measure whether the applicant is physically able to do the job	Good validity but mainly limited to unskilled or semi-skilled jobs	Danger of unfair discrimination if not used on job-related criteria
Literacy and numeracy tests	Tests that measure applicants' levels of literacy and numeracy	Good for screening applicants from school, or for unskilled workers if reading, writing or arithmetic is a core job component Good validity	Suitable for relatively few jobs
Intelligence tests	Tests that measure many different types of intellectual or cognitive functions	High validity and reliability Intelligence is linked to trainability and problem solving Intelligence is one of the most consistent personality traits across situations	Not always easy to identify the type of intelligence you want to measure Trained psychologists are needed to administer the better tests Can be expensive
Personality tests	Tests that measure personality traits	Useful if you know exactly what personality traits you are looking for and why	Trained psychologists are required to administer these tests and provide feedback Can be expensive Used in isolation, they have a poor predictive validity

Analogous tests (simulations such as intray exercises)	Tests that simulate the work the newcomer will be doing	High predictive validity but only useful for a limited number of jobs	May just indicate who has done the tasks before, or the trainability of applicants
Assessment centres	A process, rather than a place, which uses a number of selection techniques in combination	Moderate validity Also useful for staff development High 'face validity' (the validity of a test at face value – it looks like it does what it is supposed to do)	Expensive and time-consuming, as they are usually staffed by senior managers and psychologists Raises the question of how you combine the results of the diverse range of tests Assessment centres are artificial environments

You will have noticed that the most commonly used selection methods, such as the interview, tend to have low validity and reliability but that the 'best predictors', such as assessment centres, are very costly.

Stop and reflect

Think of the most recent time that you applied and were selected for a job. Which methods were used? Why do you think they were chosen? Do you think that this choice of method was sensible given the requirements of the job?

Induction

A new employee's entry into a business is crucial and, done badly, results in the high costs of the newcomer feeling unhappy, demotivated and unclear about what is expected of them. This is likely to result in poor work performance and high staff turnover, which are costly for the person and the organisation. Induction is the initial period of a newcomer's employment and involves adjusting to the new environment. During this period, newcomers are concerned about the expectations the organisation has of them, about meeting strangers with whom they must form working relationships, about loneliness, about using new technology and about being able to do the job. These concerns can cause great anxiety, which is potentially both unhealthy and unproductive. The purpose of formal organisational induction programmes is to reduce the anxiety associated with a change of environment so that newcomers can become productive as quickly as possible. Therefore, familiarisation with the job is an important part of the induction process. This familiarisation process is likely to be specific to every job, so this section will concentrate on the more general, and frequently ignored, subject of reducing the anxiety associated with a new environment.

One of the key ways of reducing this anxiety is to brief the newcomer fully about the organisation's expectations and the nature of the job – although this should already have occurred, in part, earlier in the organisational entry process. Consequently, good induction is particularly important for organisational programmes that have neither addressed the issue of developing a psychological contract nor included a realistic preview or description of the role. In these cases, anxiety is intensified as the newcomer arrives not knowing what is expected. An important research finding for organisational entry concerns the connection between high anxiety and low job satisfaction. As induction is a key period when impressions and expectations are being formed, low levels of job satisfaction experienced at this time might crystallise and become part of the newcomer's fixed attitudes regarding the job and the organisation.

It is helpful to think about the type of information and support that may be useful for a newcomer, by structuring the information into different levels, as suggested by Fowler (1996).

- Individual level – includes personal contractual issues and personal support.

  This could include basic information on: hours of work and breaks; flexitime arrangements, if any; leave; expenses; payment methods; salary increases and rewards; welfare and other benefits, such as sports and social facilities; training and development opportunities; sickness and absence procedures; geography of buildings and location of facilities; dress code.

- Job/task level – provides a general idea of the work to be done and how the employee should begin his or her employment.

  This is likely to include knowledge of: health and safety (for example, fire drills); work procedures (including, for example, security), use of telephones, data protection; other procedures and regulations; equipment and resources available, including IT resources; standards and targets for performance; on-the-job training availability; helplines and manuals.

- Support at departmental level – the relationship of the employee's job to other jobs in the department and to the jobs of people in other departments.

  This may include: meeting key contacts; defining internal customers; identifying where joint working is required; departmental objectives; departmental communications mechanisms.

- Organisational level – wider issues to do with the structure, objectives and wider context of the business as a whole.

  This could include: policies, aims and core values; HRM policies, such as discipline procedures, equal opportunities, staff development, and pension and insurance schemes; the structure and functions of the business; the nature and size of the business and its competitors.

These levels assume a large business, but they could be adapted and simplified for small ones. They do not cover everything; additional information may be needed, depending on the particular category of employee and the background and experience of the individual. But however thorough the formal induction, you need to remember that any new employee has to be socialised into becoming a full member of the organisation. This is a gradual process as no one can take in everything new that they learn all at once. They are influenced by everyone they meet, formally and informally, whether colleagues, customers or clients.

Stop and reflect

Consider your last experience of induction. Do you think it adequately prepared you for the demands of your job? Based on your subsequent experience of employment in the organisation, how could the induction have been improved?

Organisational exit

Finally, we should recognise that entering an organisation will inevitably be followed, for one reason or another, by leaving it. All organisations are likely to be aware of their attrition rate or labour turnover. Indeed, the one certainty for people working in organisations today is the certainty of change. The driving force for organisations in both the private and the public sector is the challenge that comes from operating in a competitive and often increasingly hostile environment. Given this, it is not surprising that the organisation's needs for human resources – in terms of the number of people and their competencies – will also be subject to change and that this change will sometimes require redundancies. These redundancies may be made across the organisation (what has been termed the downsizing of the organisation) or may be limited to certain newly redundant jobs.

However, exit does not happen only because of the changed needs of the organisation. People, too, may want to bring their employment to an end, for reasons that include a more attractive offer from another firm, a move to a different area for personal reasons or the decision to retire from work. In other words, exit may be a result of changing personal needs *or* the changing needs of the organisation. It can also be the end-point of a grievance or disciplinary process.

In a rapidly changing world in which employment is increasingly insecure, it is likely that both organisational entry and organisational exit will be more frequent in the lives of individuals and organisations than in the past, when, to some extent, they represented the monumental 'beginning' and 'end' to people's working lives. A high rate of turnover can be costly in finance terms as well as meaning valuable skills and experience are lost, perhaps to competitors. But it is also the case that in some organisations, very low turnover means the spread of age and experience amongst staff becomes narrow and no new ideas are introduced.

The next sections will examine the different types of organisational exit, as well as the related area of disciplinary and grievance management.

Voluntary exit

Many instances of employee exit will be voluntary: changing personal needs will lead individuals to resign from their jobs to pursue other activities or to retire. This natural 'attrition' of staff, while it may be instigated by the employee, has important consequences for the organisation. If there is no change in the organisation's need for human resources, it must ensure that recruitment and/or training programmes are in place to meet the requirement for employees with capabilities to continue to meet the organisation's objectives.

However, a sudden increase in resignations, or a level of turnover above that experienced by other companies competing for similar staff, may indicate problems that are specific to a department or general to the organisation. The more that managers can find out about the situation the better. Are many people leaving for better salaries, better prospects, more flexibilty in the work-life balance, to start their own businesses? Many organisations use exit interviews to glean further information on people's reasons for resigning. These interviews have advantages and disadvantages. On the one hand, an employee may be inclined to be more frank and open than they would otherwise be, given that they do not have to face the consequences of being associated with negative views as a continuing employee. On the other hand, the decision to leave is a major one for most people, and detailed questioning of their motives may put people on the defensive, with a consequent loss of candour.

Downsizing and redundancy

Although an organisation's need periodically to make staff redundant has been mentioned, this should not be the first stage of a redundancy programme but, rather, an outcome of an earlier stage: a review of the work that needs to be done and a comparison of the human resources needed to carry it out. Business process re-engineering is a method of reviewing the internal aspects of organisations and then rearranging them into the configuration most likely to achieve the organisation's objectives.

In practice, however, it is often regarded as a 'numbers game', with an emphasis on eliminating jobs to save costs, when, perhaps, the concentration should be upon eliminating work, by examining the rationale for doing what we do in the way that we do it. This is the business process re-engineering approach, but with the aim not of getting more from less but better from less. This approach does not avoid the need for redundancies, but it does mean that the focus is on retaining those people with the skills and competencies that will be needed in the future. It also means recognising people's skills and abilities and identifying how these can be managed in the strategic interests of the organisation, shifting the focus from redundancy to redeployment.

The need for redundancies should be related to particular areas of work, rather than represent an 'across the board' requirement. In practice, the issue is often so sensitive for organisations that they adopt a less analytical approach than the one they would take for decisions related to, for example, capital equipment. If sufficient care is not taken, organisations have found that, for example, voluntary redundancy schemes save some money in the short term but allow too much valuable experience to be lost.

One of the reasons why redundancy is so problematic for both managers and theorists is that it runs counter to much of the rhetoric of popular theories of management – in particular, those definitions of 'soft' HRM that emphasise the need to secure the commitment of employees to the organisation. It is clearly difficult to attempt to secure employee commitment to the organisation while a programme of compulsory redundancies is being implemented. Making redundancies, therefore, requires careful management if it is not to have consequences that undermine the wider people policies of the organisation and damage its external image.

Downsizing can have a devastating effect on the organisation. In some companies, one round of downsizing leads to another. It is hardly surprising that it can take some time for the organisation to recover from the trauma and regain the commitment of the staff that remains. The success of initiatives such as total quality management and **customer care**, for example, depends on staff who are highly motivated and actively working towards quality improvement for the organisation. Yet it is difficult for staff to sustain a level of commitment to the future of the company when they feel that their own future is under threat.

From the 1980s onward, moves to reduce restrictions on managers' 'right to manage' suggested that companies must have the ability to shed surplus labour and become leaner organisations. Nevertheless making people redundant still has legal implications that cannot be ignored, as well as being uncomfortable for the managers who have to implement the decisions. It is worth noting that many studies cast doubt on the espoused benefits of downsizing to firms' competitiveness. Indeed, studies of companies in the United States have shown that not all of them benefitted from downsizing. Some of the drawbacks reported were:

- smaller than anticipated increases in productivity
- reductions in costs not achieved
- increases in efficiency not achieved
- profitability not increased
- underestimates of the length of time taken for the organisation to recover from downsizing
- poor morale in the people who remain
- an increased distrust of management
- an increased resistance to further change.

In essence, the studies suggest that the difficulties involved in implementing redundancy programmes, coupled with their indirect effects on morale and motivation, combine to reduce the predicted benefits of redundancies. It could well be that in some of these companies the expectation that downsizing would solve a number of problems at a stroke was misplaced, since the emphasis was on getting rid of posts and people, rather than on reducing the amount of unproductive work. Downsizing can be a powerful corrosive on the psychological contract. Indeed, the perceived loyalty of organisations to their employees, and of employees to their organisations, have both dropped in the past decade.

Managing grievance and disciplinary procedures

Staff may leave an organisation because of disciplinary penalties or as the result of a grievance. This is fairly rare but cannot be ignored. Managers often have difficulty handling grievances and disciplinary procedures. A grievance is usually defined as a complaint that has been formally presented to an appropriate management representative or a union official. Disciplinary procedures are when a manager acts formally to enforce the rules of the organisation, such as by warning an employee that if they continue or repeat undesirable work behaviour, penalties will ensue. In other words, the employee instigates the grievance procedure while the manager starts the disciplinary processes. The two can be linked if a grievance raised by an employee concerns the behaviour of other employees. The interests of employers and employees are not always compatible, and this produces the need for systems of grievance and disciplinary resolution that are organisationally appropriate and meet the requirements of the law. Accordingly, there are both informal and formal dimensions. Employees expect to be treated in a reasonable, fair and consistent manner and to face disciplinary action only on the basis of just cause after thorough investigation. Employers expect acceptable performance. All of these expectations are shaped not only by the formal employment contract but also by the informal psychological contract.

There is a clear business interest here. If discipline and grievances are managed effectively, employee dissatisfaction should decrease and motivation increase. Labour turnover should decline and retention rates improve. However, if formal procedures are applied harshly, inconsistently or arbitrarily, then employees are likely to react adversely. Conversely, indulgent disciplinary processes may lead to widespread transgressions and make it subsequently impossible to re-establish standards.

The problem of striking the correct balance is further complicated given the HRM emphasis on line management involvement in employee relations. The process of outsourcing, de-layering and downsizing found in many contemporary organisations has sometimes resulted in the absence of any human resource specialist, leaving line managers who are lacking support and expert advice (Thornhill and Saunders, 1998). Human resources departments can be too 'hands off', not wishing to get involved in operational issues (Proctor and Currie, 1999). For some line managers, human resource issues get sacrificed when the pressure from operational issues is extreme.

Greater emphasis on training managers in handling formal procedures is required. Where a dismissal has been challenged at an employment tribunal, the tribunal will test the issue of 'fairness' and 'reasonableness' by considering whether the disciplinary procedures that the employer has applied 'conform to the concepts of natural justice'. Therefore, it is important that such procedures exist and are widely understood and followed by all concerned parties and, moreover, that they are integrated with other human resource policies.

Accordingly, all managers involved in managing discipline or grievance need to be aware of the negative consequences that can arise. Poor practice can have severe implications for the employment relationship and the legitimacy of management in any organisation. There are five main tests that, according to Renwick and Gennard, management must pass if they are to manage grievance and discipline issues effectively (2001, pp. 168–91). These are:

- fairness
- reasonableness
- consistency
- operating with just cause
- operating within the law.

Renwick and Gennard point out that if these standards are not upheld, then managers may find that their practices will be subject to legal intervention.

3.3: Performance and rewards

In the previous section we looked at the organisational entry process as the first stage in a series of functional activities involved in managing human resources. Of course, the interest of managers in a new employee does not stop once the induction process is complete. If employees are taken on in order to contribute to the organisation's objectives, it seems clear that there must be systems in place to assess the extent of that contribution and promote continuing high performance. Several tools contribute to making this possible. They include monitoring performance, managing pay and rewards (which as we saw in Chapter 2 are influential in motivating high performance) and developing people through training, coaching, mentoring and counselling. These activities are sometimes grouped together under the heading 'managing performance', which refers to a set of techniques and procedures that share the common characteristics of:

- providing information on the contribution of human resources to the wider objectives of the organisation
- forming a framework of techniques to secure the maximum achievement of objectives for given inputs
- providing a means of inspecting the functioning of the process that delivers performance against objectives.

However, just as many organisations have devolved responsibility for recruitment and selection to line managers following the movement towards HRM, many performance management functions are now in the hands of a combination of both line managers and human resource specialists.

Performance is commonly evaluated through a formal process of appraisal. As you will see in the following, one of the key issues of performance appraisal is to find a way of measuring employees' performance accurately. In other words, a method should be valid (i.e., it is a true representation of that person's performance), reliable (i.e., it is not just a picture of that person's performance on a bad day or a good day) and objective (it does not depend on who is doing the assessing).

This section will examine some of the issues involved in monitoring and controlling performance, using the idea of the control loop and a focus on performance appraisal as a vehicle for monitoring and managing performance.

The control loop

A useful way of thinking about managing performance is through the concept of a **control loop**. The loop involves three main stages: setting specific targets; monitoring the extent to which individuals fulfil these targets; and taking corrective action if and as necessary. A fourth stage may be added if desired: setting new targets in the light of previous performance.

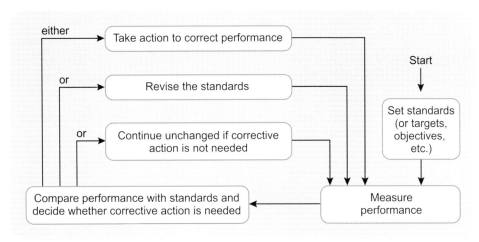

Figure 3.3: The control loop

In the context of managing performance, one of the theoretical bases of the control loop is goal-setting theory, which was first put forward by the social psychologist Edwin Locke (see Locke et al., 1981). As discussed in Chapter 2, Locke argued that goals pursued by employees can play an important role in motivating superior performance. In aiming to achieve goals, people examine the consequences of their behaviour. If they think their current behaviour will not allow them to achieve their goals, they will either modify their behaviour or choose different goals. If managers can intervene to set goals in such a way that individuals think the organisation's aims are worth achieving, then they should be able to improve their staff's performance.

However, this analysis of performance management assumes that management is, in essence, a rational activity. It assumes implicitly that:

- an organisation's goals can be expressed in terms clear enough that they can be used to construct actual policies, standards and targets

- it is possible to measure – or at least estimate reliably – the extent to which an individual or a group is helping to achieve those standards and targets

- human performance can be analysed as a series of interlocking causes and effects

- this series can be managed – in other words, poorly performing parts of the chain can be 'repaired', or at least 'improved', by the actions of 'managers'.

Throughout this section, the extent to which this rationalist model of performance applies in real situations will be considered.

The day-to-day managerial control of human resources is often much more 'messy' than the rational model suggests. Very few managers work to a detailed and specific plan. Often their objectives are numerous and sometimes contradictory (for example, some organisations have a commitment to investing in people at the same time as making redundancies). Also, objectives may be changing so fast that any attempt to base a system of performance management on them would be problematic.

Even when objectives are clearly defined, the precise standards to be attained and maintained to achieve them may not be so clearly specified. Some strategic goals, such as increasing sales in a certain country, have an implicit measure of performance associated with them, but with others – for example, increasing customer satisfaction – it may be hard to think of how to measure performance satisfactorily. Sometimes, the kind of performance that is measured is chosen not because it is the most valuable definition for the organisation but because it is simply easier to measure.

Critics of the rational approach to performance management also argue that taking too mechanistic a view of the management of people undermines the social and informal basis of relationships at work, which depend on interpersonal interactions.

One of the key implications of the control loop as a framework for managing human resources is that there should be standards against which an individual can be assessed. However, managers must be cautious about their expectations for measurement and must consider the possibility of 'objective' measures (based on independently verifiable data) and the inevitability of subjective measures (derived from human judgement). For example, objective measures are usually quantitative measures of how well an individual or a group is meeting the objectives set. They might specify targets, such as deadlines, quantities, costs and resource usage. However, objective measures may not be as robust as they appear. Although numerical measures may, on the face of it, seem incontrovertible, further scrutiny may reveal that this is not the case. For example, profitability would seem to be a tried and tested measure, yet accountants know that profits reflect decisions on how to treat costs and revenues and on when paper gains should be released onto the profit-and-loss account. In other words, many apparently objective measures are, in reality, quite subjective.

Subjective measures of performance are inevitably made in all organisations. Most people will have a complex picture of the abilities and performance of their colleagues, which is based only in part on formal results. These subjective assessments may be useful in deciding who to promote, for example. If subjective assessments are carefully and systematically formed, they may offer a more accurate gauge of performance than so-called objective measures.

However, subjective measures are associated with a variety of problems. Because ratings are given by people to other people, it can be hard to disentangle social influences: ratings may reflect race, gender or personal biases rather than pure performance. In addition, it is a well-understood finding that many appraisers feel socially uncomfortable giving relatively poor ratings. As a result, they may give ratings tightly clustered around the mean, or give way to a general rating 'creep' by awarding more marks above a suggested mean than below it.

Performance appraisals

Performance is usually measured in organisations through a process of appraisal. In some cases, people see appraisal as merely form-filling and submit passively to the process as part of the organisation's routines. In others, it can be more negatively interpreted as a system for maintaining top-down control by closely monitoring output. At their best, however, performance appraisals go beyond this and serve a variety of purposes within an organisation. Although they are frequently used to inform individuals of the extent to which objectives are being met and to update these objectives or agree upon new ones, appraisals can also provide an opportunity to discuss an individual's performance at work in its entirety, perhaps including the suitability of the given objectives. Appraisals may provide an opportunity to consider an employee's future 'direction' and development needs.

The aims for appraisal systems therefore should include the following:

- objective setting, to clarify and agree on goals for a given future period
- evaluating, to enable the organisation to share out the money, promotions and rewards fairly
- auditing, to discover the work potential, both present and future, of individuals and departments
- discovering training needs by identifying gaps and inadequacies that could be remedied through training programmes
- motivating staff to reach organisational standards and objectives
- developing individuals by advice, information and the exploration of changing behaviour and practice
- checking the effectiveness of personnel procedures and practices
- building relationships between staff and managers
- constructing succession plans for human resources, and departmental and corporate planning.

Trying to realise this multiplicity of purposes means paying considerable attention both to the construction and integration of a performance appraisal scheme as a whole and to the way in which it is managed by everyone involved. Many organisations are trying to transform their appraisal systems into one based on a shared process in which the emphasis is on mutual development rather than one-way judgements. This means that the manager is faced with multiple responsibilities and demands. These are not just to be the appraisers, but also to sustain and monitor the extent to which the scheme is consonant with the wider human resource programmes and purposes of the organisation.

Appraisal is usually conducted by an employee's line manager, and this continues to be the most common pattern. However, with the reduction in the number of management layers and the increasing flexibility of jobs in organisations, this may now be proving more difficult. A manager may have too many subordinates to deal with or see them too infrequently to be in a position to evaluate their performance. Furthermore, employees may be working on projects that overlap with different managers and departments, or be moving around different jobs, so that they may have several line managers.

There has been a variety of responses to these problems, and research has reported an increasing use of alternative sources of information, in particular from peers, subordinates and customers (Redman, 2005). Peer appraisal is still rather uncommon in organisations, although in theory it could have much to offer because peers may be in a position to give a unique insight into an individual's team contribution. Upward appraisal – the appraisal of line managers by their subordinates – while not yet very common, is a practice that is also increasing (Redman, 2005). Many organisations are moving towards a notion of '360-degree' appraisals, when a cross section of colleagues and even customers are asked to comment on the performance of an individual.

With the increasing focus on customer and quality in many organisations, 'satisfying the customer' has become a key dimension of staff evaluation, and customers themselves have been drawn into the appraisal process in different ways – for example, through customer questionnaires that are then used in staff appraisal or the practice of using 'mystery shoppers'. It is often argued that **360-degree feedback** appraisal provides a more objective and accurate picture of a person's performance, as it draws on different sources of evaluation and perspectives; however, as Grint (1993) suggests, this may just involve replacing the subjective assessment of a single appraiser with the subjective assessments of multiple assessors.

In summary, there is a good deal of evidence to suggest that formal appraisal interviews are generally neither well conducted nor well received (e.g. Grint, 1993; Coates, 2000). Appraisers often feel it necessary to reinforce their place in the hierarchy and thereby increase their superiority over the appraisee. Despite efforts to ensure that assessments are made on objective and quantifiable grounds, appraisers may still be influenced by their personal relationships with the appraisee. Moreover appraisees often feel that their performance is being assessed during the appraisal interview more intensively than at any other time. They may therefore frequently say what they feel the appraiser wants to hear. In some cases, this leads to people over-extending themselves when agreeing objectives for the future. This, in turn, can lead to stress and underperformance as the extent of the over-commitment gradually becomes apparent.

This discussion of appraiser style points to potential conflicts when the same appraisal system is used for both judgmental and developmental purposes (Redman, 2005). Appraisal systems are often criticised for being made to serve incompatible ends, placing conflicting demands on both appraisers and appraisees. Finally, McGivern and Ferlie (2007) argue that yet another common interpretation of performance appraisal is that it is no more than box ticking, something that has to be gone through but has little relevance or impact.

Stop and reflect

Do you recognise any of these problems of appraisal from your own experience? Do you think it is possible to reconcile the conflicting demands made of appraisal systems?

Performance management

Managers do not only monitor performance through appraisals, as these are usually done only once or twice a year. Ensuring effective management control requires that action is taken when there is a difference between planned and actual performance. Three options are possible: continuing unchanged; taking action to correct or improve performance; or revising the standard. In reality, of course, a manager may respond to a problem with a mixture of all three.

Continuing unchanged

Monitoring may suggest that not only is an individual not going to meet his or her objectives but also that there are reasons why the best option might be to avoid taking corrective action. For example, it might be that the disparity is not serious at this point and intervention can be postponed. Moreover, it should not be assumed that intervention will always result in positive outcomes. In some circumstances, it could actually make things worse.

Correcting performance

This option might involve insisting that the work is done again or improved, arranging additional training for some of the staff – or any other form of corrective action. The manager has to consider whether corrective action is being applied directly to the cause of the problem or to the effect arising from that cause. On some occasions, it may even be that discipline (e.g. formal warnings) may need to be enforced to ensure that standards are not undermined or ignored. This will require considering many aspects of working with people, including leadership, motivation, power, conflict and disciplinary procedures. You may also need to consider possible legal implications.

Revising the standard

Here it may be decided by the manager that the original goal was not appropriate and needs modifying. The standard or target may need revision when a standard is exceeded or when changed circumstances have made the standard (or target) unrealistic. However, revising standards can produce a number of adverse and unanticipated consequences. These include: encouraging people to ignore any future standards; discouraging those who worked hard to meet the target; engendering a feeling of failure. There is also no guarantee that the new standard will be any more realistic than before.

It is important, however, that individuals have their performance monitored for reasons other than those associated with control. There is, as we have seen, an important development aspect of appraisal, and employees will often feel more secure and valued in their work when they receive constructive feedback on their performance either informally as part of day-to-day management or as part of the formal appraisal system.

Performance management usually goes hand in hand with the reward system of an organisation. You should recall that HRM emphasises an integrated approach to the management of personnel. Consequently, managing rewards (as informed by performance management) can be used to support organisational objectives. Under HRM, payment systems are generally not just seen as a cost, or as compensation for past service rendered, but are used as a managerial tool to produce certain effects: to motivate, to retain, to control or as a way to engineer strategic or cultural change. For example, many appraisal systems seek to ensure not only that employees achieve specific job-related outputs but also that they demonstrate attitudes and values that are consistent with the wider organisational culture. Judging this is likely to be subjective and requires good people skills from the appraiser.

Therefore, relating pay to performance is an important strand of HRM philosophy. Systems of **performance related pay (PRP)** have been advocated as a way of strengthening employees' motivation and identification with the organisation. In particular, individual schemes of PRP are seen as potentially eliciting commitment in several ways. The criteria used in appraisal and PRP are usually derived from corporate objectives and 'missions' and therefore can serve to shape individuals' behaviours and attitudes towards those valued by the organisation. The next section looks at the place of PRP in HRM in more detail.

Performance related pay

Collective bargaining has declined in importance since the early 1980s, and many organisations have introduced more diverse sets of pay policies. This may be due to the rise of the flexible firm, discussed earlier. In particular, there has been a marked increase in the incidence of performance related pay. PRP refers to a range of payment systems that share the common characteristic of linking employees' income to either their own performance, that of their work group or that of the organisation as a whole. As we saw earlier, appraisal can be based on individual outputs (e.g. sales, measures of customer satisfaction or quality of service) or measures of competencies or skills (inputs). Traditionally, the linkage between performance and pay increases has been reserved for managerial positions. However, PRP is now becoming more widespread throughout organisations (Lewis, 2001).

See Chapter 2, for expectancy, instrumentality and valence.

Applying expectancy theory from Chapter 2 to PRP suggests that it would stand to reason that three conditions must be met if people are to work harder:

- People must feel that their behaviour affects the performance of the relevant group (expectancy).
- They must be convinced that any improved performance will bring them the reward of a higher PRP pay-out.
- Employees must value the bonus pay.

This means that if people believe that by supplying more effort they will receive a valuable pay-out from a PRP scheme, they are more likely to work harder than if they believe any of these relationships are slight or uncertain.

A crucial issue when evaluating different payment systems is that of perceived equity and fairness. For example, according to Adams's equity theory (1963) discussed in Chapter 2, people will formulate a ratio between their inputs into the job (experience, effort, skills) and outputs (e.g. salary, benefits, promotion, recognition) and compare it with the perceived ratio for other people in the same or similar situation. Thus, when we discuss different payment systems, we need to bear in mind the issue of perceived (in)equity.

PRP and appraisal

PRP obviously depends on an appraisal system and is open to the same problems and criticisms that were reviewed earlier. However, perceived distortion, bias and inequity in the assessment process can create particularly severe problems when appraisal is related to pay. Lewis (2001) suggests that, in theory, PRP is introduced in order to serve various objectives besides the traditional one of 'motivating':

- to help in recruitment and retention by offering higher salaries to high performers
- to weaken the power of trade unions – PRP serves to bypass the collective bargaining process, in which trade unions are often involved, and to individualise pay
- to increase the role of line managers – through the introduction of PRP, line managers have to pay greater attention to communicating with, monitoring and evaluating their staff
- to provide greater financial control by rewarding those who are contributing to the performance of the organisation
- to reward and recognise good performance; this is especially important in downsized, down-layered organisations where promotion may not be easy even for good performers
- to support programmes of cultural change – PRP puts a financial tag on the values the organisation wants to promote and is a way of communicating these values to employees, as well as rewarding them for displaying 'appropriate' behaviours and attitudes.

However, empirical studies suggest that PRP may actually have little impact on performance and motivation in practice and, in some cases, can have a negative influence (Randell 1997; Roberts, 1997). There are several reasons for this.

First, the difference in pay between high and low performers may not be meaningful. In other words, high performers may not think that their additional reward reflects their additional efforts. Indeed, financial constraints may limit the extent to which performance can be rewarded; as a result, PRP can lead to very small differentials in pay between high and low performers. Employees may feel insulted by the low level of extra pay they receive. It has also been suggested that PRP could inhibit innovation and change and encourage employees to 'stick to what they know' and can do well, concentrating on those aspects of the job that are assessed at the expense of other, perhaps less tangible, aspects. Employees may also be reluctant to engage in innovative practices in case their efforts are not acknowledged and their assessment is adversely affected.

Second, by rewarding some individuals and not others, PRP could endanger cohesion and cooperation among colleagues. To counter these effects, some companies have incorporated factors such as 'contribution to team-working' in their appraisal criteria. Further, there may not be any clear link between employees' performance and pay. Employees may not feel that their pay increase is actually closely linked to their own performance; they may believe that performance measures do not reflect their actual performance. This can especially be the case when performance is measured by superiors, or is perceived to be biased or distorted or may depend on factors not under the control of the individual. Consequently, PRP systems may place the blame for poor performance on individuals' shoulders when broader factors in the organisation or the environment are at fault.

Finally, PRP assumes a rather simplistic view of motivation and the psychological contract. In truth, individuals are motivated by a wide range of factors. Implying that the manipulation of pay alone will be motivating is simplistic and in some cases insulting. Some people may not be especially motivated by money as a reward. Everyone may not think in the way expectancy theory implies: rather than determining their actions by weighing up the rewards on offer, they may be happy to conform to group norms almost irrespective of the outcome. Etzioni (1988) has argued that, in practice, people behave according to their values, rather than as the rational calculating machine that underlies process theories of motivation.

If an overall conclusion can be drawn from studies of PRP, it is that careful work design must precede the introduction of a scheme if it is to be effective. The evidence of the effectiveness of PRP in boosting performance is mixed.

Stop and reflect

Do you think flexible systems of pay are the best way of motivating excellent performance in organisations? From your own experience what problems have emerged from the use of performance related pay?

3.4: Developing human resources

You may well have recognised that, in the last two decades, training and development has been high on the political and managerial agenda. The increased interest in training and development throughout the major economies of the world has been driven by the belief that training and development can influence performance and competitiveness. Accordingly, training and development is central to the philosophy of HRM. HRM sees employees as a key resource for achieving organisational competitiveness (or maximum effectiveness in the public sector), and so it follows that employee development is a means through which organisational strategy and individual behaviour can be aligned.

As was shown in the previous section, regular appraisals often highlight obstacles to an employee's ability to contribute fully to the objectives of the organisation. Some of these obstacles may centre on the employee lacking the skills needed to perform well and indicate an opportunity to use training and development to acquire the missing skills. Even organisations that have managed to recruit and select highly skilled people are unlikely to be able to ignore the need to train and develop their staff: skills need updating, new skills must be learned and people may find themselves doing work that is very different from what they did when they first joined the organisation.

Developing human resources can be seen as an investment decision on the part of the organisation. It spends time and money now in the expectation that the returns on the investment – be they in terms of higher productivity, improved quality or greater flexibility – will more than outweigh the initial cost. However, just as with other investments, spending money for the sake of it is unlikely to produce returns that make the exercise viable. Investment in people needs to be as carefully thought out and aligned with objectives as with any other investment.

Investing in people through training and development has a special status, however. Not only can training contribute to the organisation's ability to achieve its objectives, but it can transform the lives and prospects of the individuals who benefit from it. Many prospective employees will judge whether to work for an organisation partly on the opportunities for advancement the organisation will afford them, and a significant proportion of those opportunities are provided by training and development.

Training and development is therefore central to the philosophy and practice of HRM. An organisation's training provision will show whether it is treating its employees as a resource rather than a cost or commodity, or in other words, whether it is actually practising HRM. For training and development to be effective, therefore, it should be viewed as an integral part of the organisation's strategy.

This section will consider the importance of training and development for both the organisation and its employees. The section will set out some of the key decisions that you, as a manager, must take in planning training and development, and offer some frameworks that are used to analyse training needs. It will be important to recognise some of the pitfalls and misconceptions that affect this area of HRM, to encourage you to take a critical approach to some of the prescriptions that are often offered.

Investing in human capital

Economists argue that the decision to spend resources – time and money – on training and developing people should be a rational one, comparable with the decision to invest, for example, in the latest capital equipment. Training and development is intended to increase the productivity of the individual or group being trained, so investment in these activities may be desirable to the extent that the costs incurred will be less than the value of the increased performance expected. This intuitively straightforward way of thinking about training and development, which was most authoritatively advanced by Becker (1975) in his book *Human Capital*, has important implications that go beyond the immediately intuitive aspects.

The first implication is the need for information. If managers are to be able to decide whether to propose a training programme, they need to know both the cost of that programme and also, in financial terms, the value it will yield. Companies devote considerable attention to collecting and gathering information to help them make well-informed decisions on investments in capital equipment, including estimates of future income streams translated into a single cash sum through a discounted cash flow. Yet, traditionally, HRM has benefitted much less from this kind of financial analysis. Here the strategic emphasis of HRM seeks to address this deficiency.

The emphasis on information focuses attention on which particular training and development activities will be profitable. Not all such activities will immediately or directly improve the productivity or flexibility of the organisation so, rather than having an overall training budget, the human capital approach implies that each proposal for an activity (e.g. a training course) should be considered on its merits. Another important consideration is the mobility of capital. In investing in its employees, a company is building the human capital in each of them. It will often be equipping employees with a mixture of firm-specific skills, which relate to the particular techniques used by the company, and also developing more general skills. General skills will be attractive to other employers, so an employee may decide to quit the company that has provided the training and accept a higher wage from another company eager to make use of his or her skills. Therefore, human capital theory highlights the need to take into account the possibility that investment in general skills may lead to employees being poached by competitors before the organisation has had a chance to recoup the cost of the training.

Moreover, the more fluid the labour market, the more difficult it will be for companies to protect the value of investments in general skills. The fact that an individual's position in the labour market is enhanced by the general skills they possess underlines the view that training and development are not the exclusive responsibility of the employer. People should be expected to invest in themselves using the same criteria that firms use – that is, will they recoup their costs in terms of future earnings potential or satisfaction. There are several ways in which people can bear some of the cost of training in general skills. For example, some professional occupations or trades pay employees significantly less during a training period or an apprenticeship than in their subsequent employment – effectively sharing the cost of training with the employee.

Although the human capital approach to training and development carries powerful implications, many practitioners find that it over-rationalises decisions taken in organisations and that, in practice, managers do not have access to the information required, such as the expected effect of a particular training course on someone's productivity.

Decisions to invest in training and development go beyond ensuring that people understand, say, the new budgeting procedures. They can also be a way of promoting an organisation's values. For example, a charity working to protect the welfare of children and young people needs staff who can detect and prevent child abuse. The staff training programme has to cultivate these skills. But it should also seek to convey and develop some of the values that inform the organisation's approach to child welfare and working with families. These might include a respect for differences, the importance of empowering those the agency works with and affirming their own efforts and aspirations. These values inform the content of courses and how they are taught. In addition, the organisation devolves responsibility for their own development to members of staff, and recognises their prior knowledge and experience in an effort to practise what it preaches. In these ways, the organisation aims both to develop the competencies that are needed and to reinforce its own central values.

It follows that staff training and development can play a vital role as part of a broader strategy of organisational change. For example, training sessions can be used to promote new approaches in order to improve interdepartmental relations, to encourage staff to come to terms with the need for change and to devise their own solutions to new challenges. In considering staff training and development, managers are often concerned not just with individual learning but also with broader processes of team and organisational learning.

Training and the knowledge economy

The emphasis on the importance of training and development to competitiveness has been strongly linked to the idea of the 'knowledge economy'. For example, Felstead et al. (2007) argue that policymakers appear to believe that 'learning', 'training' and 'skills' are the key levers to enhance productivity and raise living standards. For many observers, the new economy is a knowledge economy, where intelligence and education are rewarded and valued as never before. Workers in the new economy are supposed to be 'self-programmable', adaptable, flexible and able to engage in self-learning (Castells, 2000). The assumption that a skilled workforce is required to produce quality goods and services is reflected in the UK government's policies on competitiveness and economic growth:

> The future of the country's prosperity lies in the knowledge economy. This is as true of the manufacturing sector as it is of the service sector. We must strive to innovate, to produce high quality, value-added products and services. And to do this, we have to ensure the right skills to support growth.

> (Patricia Hewitt, quoted in DCSF, 2003)

Within the European Union (EU), the Lisbon summit of 2000 set a strategic target for the EU to become the world's leading 'knowledge economy'. It specified the key conditions for achieving this goal as being the upgrading of skills, a high level of participation in life-long learning and the promotion of high-quality jobs.

However, a balanced view of this must be taken. Despite the popularisation of the concept of the knowledge economy among researchers and politicians, empirical evidence concerning employment trends suggests that most jobs do not require skilled people to carry them out (Felstead et al., 2007, p. 104). This suggests that the much hoped-for 'knowledge economy' may be some way distant. In a similar vein, Korczynski (2005) argues that front-line service work – for example, homecare assistants, restaurant waiters, retail store workers and call-centre workers – is a major area of employment growth but remains some distance removed from the knowledge economy. He argues, 'The rhetoric concerning the "high skill" economy is amazingly adept at avoiding the fact that the largest area of growth is in poorly rewarded frontline service jobs' (Korczynski, 2005, p. 3).

Therefore, while it might be the case that the people performing these low-skill jobs are themselves increasingly qualified (and with the recession and downturn in graduate recruitment programmes, this is likely to become increasingly so), this does not mean that the jobs themselves or the economy are moving towards a requirement for 'high skill'. Intensified globalised competition in service industries means not just an increase in competition based on service quality, but also an increase in price-based competition. For Korczynski (2005), this means that management will need skills that lead to service quality, but will need to minimise the costs involved in creating these skills. This sounds very much like a scenario for a continued, and intensified, use of low-cost skills.

Finally, while the introduction of technology and shifting customer demands may have some impact on skills, this is not always a positive relationship. For example, the development of computers has created highly skilled jobs for analysts and programmers, but it has also deskilled those whose expertise depended on what went before. Nor is work that involves computers necessarily highly skilled. Call-centres are extremely technologically sophisticated workplaces, but few could be considered sites of 'knowledge work'.

The central point is that technology, market forces or flexibility do not inevitably support skills development. There are choices to be made about the ways that work is designed, monitored and controlled, and these choices will affect skills in a range of ways.

Stop and reflect

Consider your working life over the last ten years. How have you upgraded your skills? What role did your manager play in this? To what extent have the requirements of work become more demanding? In contrast, have some jobs been 'deskilled'?

Recognising development needs

It has been noted in this chapter that there is a growing tendency for activities that were once the preserve of personnel specialists to be shared with, or even transferred to, line managers. This is especially true of training and development. As attention has focused on the value of companies' investment in human capital, so all managers are increasingly being charged with developing and maintaining this investment. The days when specialist training departments had exclusive responsibility for ensuring that employees were equipped with appropriate skills are fast receding. So while in some organisations, a specialist department may take the lead in identifying commonly occurring training needs, determining cost-effective means of meeting those needs, monitoring the progress of staff development plans and policies, and advising and assisting line managers in the development of individual staff, it is the individual's line manager who now bears most of the responsibility for identifying and fulfilling training needs. It is the line manager who knows the person's work and previous experience and aspirations and is therefore uniquely placed to assist in that person's development.

Staff development need not mean additional activities; it is rather an aspect of activities that happen anyway. The term the 'learning organisation' has been used to describe the kind of ethos that can develop within organisations. If on-the-job training is approached in an atmosphere of encouragement, and if people are regularly willing to take risks, to challenge each other and to learn from their mistakes, this can result in a climate within the department or organisation in which development opportunities are sought after, rather than avoided.

However, some development needs must be anticipated. Consider the following situations.

- A large UK bank decides to merge with another in France to create one of the largest banks in Europe.
- The financial arm of a major retailer decides to launch its own investment fund.
- A group of employees buys out their business from the company that has owned it for years.

The common feature in all these situations is that they involve transitions – either by an organisation or by an individual. Transitions of this sort are familiar and, to some extent, even predictable. For example, organisations (and projects) go through phases of formation, growth, establishment and maturity; or they decide to undertake a different type of work; or they adopt a new policy demanding new skills and making new demands on staff. Likewise, an individual's involvement within an organisation often goes through several different stages and the individual becomes responsible for a wider range of activities. The more clear-cut the transition, the more likely it is that those involved will appreciate – and request – the chance to learn skills that will help them in their new or future role, or to share experiences with others in comparable situations.

While you will have noted the emphasis given in HRM to adopting a more strategic approach to training and development, the question remains of how training and development programmes are to be formulated and implemented. You can consider many questions. Who should take ownership of this process – human resource professionals or line managers? How should the training needs be identified and fulfilled? What are the most appropriate methods to use? Some of these questions will be considered in the following section.

Training needs analysis

If people have been doing something for many years, they may think that the difficulties they experience are inevitable. Nevertheless, in most cases people will welcome an opportunity to make their work easier, or to do it better. A managerial assessment of training needs is not to be made in isolation. The individual concerned will also make their own assessment and so will their colleagues. However, the manager should try to negotiate an agreeable set of outcomes, balancing their needs and preferences with those created by the situation. Appraisals may be a suitable time for this because they represent an opportunity to consider a person's work in its entirety as well as the whole person (their strengths and weaknesses and 'the fit' to their job). It is also a scheduled occasion when the manager can ask appraisees to collect their own thoughts, analyse their own performance and make a more detached assessment.

Undertaking a **training needs analysis (TNA)** involves a number of stages. The first is identifying what the job involves through discussions with the jobholder and those with whom they deal: the job purpose, areas of responsibility and the key activities and tasks. Second, the competencies, knowledge and (often) attitudes that are required to do the job must be determined, distinguishing as far as possible between those that are essential and those that are desirable. Third, a profile of the existing skills of the person doing the job, on the basis of their past experience, qualifications and demonstrated ability in the workplace, is drawn up. These are matched with the list of the knowledge, skills and attitudes required. If a significant gap is apparent between the required job and the existing skills – especially if a skill is important for that job – then this is identified as a training need.

Such an approach has important benefits. It is systematic, and so helps to prevent jumping to the wrong conclusions. It also helps set priorities for varied training needs that are based on organisational requirements. However, this approach works best with well-defined jobs that require specific skills or techniques that can be reliably cultivated in people who are willing to acquire them.

There are, however, also factors that may complicate the use of this approach:

- The work is unstructured and rather fluid. In addition, the smaller the organisation, the less specialised and defined will be the roles.
- The skills and knowledge may not be obvious from lists of the key activities. It may not be easy to train a person in the abilities required.
- People who offer particular skills may resent being told they are 'deficient' and need training; the organisation might do better to fit the role to what the person can offer.

For these reasons, a formal training needs analysis will not always be fruitful or appropriate. Moreover, there is a further problem: how does a person judge his or her existing abilities in his or her work? The obvious thing to do is to assume that people are not very good at the things they find difficult, but identifying training needs on this basis can be problematic. Therefore, it is often necessary to canvass a number of opinions on the work being assessed. A multi-perspective approach often proves more successful than relying on the assessment of the jobholder.

Planning and designing training programmes

This process involves choosing from a range of on-the-job and off- This process involves choosing from a range of on-the-job and off-the-job training methods. On-the-job training is probably the most common approach and can range from relatively unsophisticated 'observe and copy' methods to highly structured programmes of job rotation, shadowing and mentoring. Overall, the main benefits of on-the-job training are that it facilitates the transfer of learning (learning is relevant) and involves limited cost. The limitations are that its effectiveness depends on trainers' (mentors, line managers) skills and willingness, it can be disruptive and in practice it is often haphazard (Doyle, 2001; Holden, 2001). Off-the-job training can take different forms, from informational methods (such as lectures, open/distance learning courses) to experiential methods (such as role playing or outdoor-based learning like an 'outward bound' course). The main advantage of off-the-job training is that it may be helpful to get people away from their work environment to facilitate exposure to new ideas. The main problems with these methods, though, are that, unlike on-the-job training, it may be difficult to transfer the new skills and knowledge acquired to the job situation, and off-the-job training tends to be expensive.

The appropriateness of any training method will depend on the fit between the method and the needs it is trying to meet. Factors such as the size of the organisation, the number of people involved and the complexity of what needs to be learned will be important. However, all methods have particular strengths and weaknesses that will be briefly examined in the following.

Learning by doing

Sometimes referred to as 'sitting by Nellie', where a new employee is put next to an experienced employee (in this term, given the name 'Nellie') to pick up how to do the job through a combination of trying it out, observation and guidance from an experienced worker. These are commonly used methods and when done well they can ensure that initial training closely meets the needs of the organisation. Unfortunately, problems arise when 'Nellie' (the experienced employee), although extremely competent in her (or his) job, is not skilled in training. This can lead to frustrations for both parties, as one struggles to understand explanations and the other cannot understand why it is taking so long to pick up skills that they take for granted.

Mentoring and coaching

This is an approach whereby a senior or experienced employee facilitates the development of a new employee. This association is wider than the trainee–trainer relationship and means that the mentor acts as an adviser and helper to the trainee throughout an extended period of development. This term is also used when an established employee is to be developed to a more advanced level, such as a junior manager being selected as having great potential and given a very senior mentor.

Shadowing and job rotation

Shadowing is usually used for management development and aims to widen the trainee's organisational experience by assigning them to periods of working with managers in different departments. However, the success of this method strongly depends on the commitment of both parties. Trainees might consider the experience as not relating to their direct work responsibilities and therefore time not well spent. Also, the receiving department might find hosting the trainee disruptive to their work.

Job rotation is a similar method. This is where workers are switched to different roles within the organisation. Job rotation derived from the 'Quality of Working Life' movement in the 1970s and was intended to help relieve boredom and thereby raise the productivity of shop-floor workers. If workers are adequately trained for their different roles then job rotation is an excellent method of achieving greater team-working and empowerment at work. However, in the absence of adequate preparation, workers may feel that they are simply being asked to do more work without being adequately compensated.

Courses and training programmes

Sometimes it helps to remove people from the day-to-day demands of their working environment so that they have the time and space necessary to think innovatively or approach problems from new perspectives. Moreover, new knowledge does not necessarily have to be directly and immediately applicable to be valuable.

Nevertheless, such courses or workshops will inevitably be interpreted in different ways by organisational members. For example, being sent on a course might be seen as a sign of approval that the training is necessary as preparation for a promotion. However, it could also be considered as a 'message' that the employee is inefficient in their work. External courses and other forms of off-the-job training have been frequently criticised, for example employees who fail to see the relevance of the training to their day-to-day work are inclined to dismiss it as a waste of time and money.

Training evaluation

Finally, it is important to recognise that training is conducted for a reason, and therefore it is necessary to consider how the effectiveness of training, both strategically and in terms of the efficacy of particular methods, is to be assessed. This part of the process is often ignored. Much literature argues that evaluation is one of the most important yet commonly neglected aspects of training and development (Holden, 2001). Evaluation is often seen as a peripheral element of training, yet it is necessary to ensure its effectiveness. If training is not assessed, it is difficult to prove that it has been worthwhile and hence to convince anyone that the investment should be repeated. It must be remembered that the interest of the individual in seeking opportunity and self-development need not necessarily accord with organisational goals and targets. Moreover, is it really possible to quantifiably 'measure' whether a training and development intervention has added 'value' to human capital?

Despite these difficulties, training effectiveness should be examined at several levels:

- Reaction: this taps trainees' views of the training programme. A familiar type of evaluation at this level is the post-course questionnaire. The problem with this level of analysis is that it evaluates the course itself, but not participants' actual learning.

- Learning: do the trainees show evidence that they have achieved the learning objectives? Here the evaluation would focus on the extent to which trainees can demonstrate that they have learned relevant concepts, knowledge and skills. This could be measured through pre- and post-training tests. While the evaluation of learning is useful, it remains incomplete: trainees may have learned and understood new concepts and ideas but not transferred these to the workplace. The transfer from learning to behaviour is the focus of the next level of evaluation.

- Behaviour: at this level, the evaluation is concerned with assessing the impact of training on behaviour. It involves comparing trainees' behaviour before and after training and assessing the extent to which their performance has improved. This could be done through performance appraisal.

- Organisational results: the extent to which training has had an impact on organisational effectiveness. Information can be collected on a wide range of organisational measures, such as customer satisfaction, productivity, staff turnover or quality improvements. However, this level of evaluation is particularly difficult since any change in these organisation-wide measures could have been brought about by factors other than training.

Problems and difficulties of training and development

The idea of developing people is full of positive associations. It fits well with the mission and values of many organisations, particularly those that are service-orientated or that emphasise the importance of their 'people' to achieving competitive advantage. Moreover, it is an aspect of management that many people, once they start attending to it, find immensely rewarding. However, problems can emerge.

Several commentators have argued that the relationships between training, commitment and performance are far more complex than suggested in the prescriptive literature. It is difficult to establish a direct causal relationship between training and performance. For example, Wong et al. (1997) in a study of small and medium-sized companies taking part in a management development programme, suggest that the effects of training were affected by a host of factors (for example, the local labour market, structure, growth stage, size of the company) and argue that the impact of training on 'the bottom line' is difficult to measure. Antonacopoulou (2001) also warns against assuming some simple and direct relationships between training, learning and performance. She argues that competing priorities and objectives (between individual employees and the organisation, or between short-term and long-term objectives) may undermine the effectiveness of training in encouraging learning, development or improved performance.

The effect of training and development on employees' attitudes and commitment is also complex. Heyes and Stuart (1996) argue that training has the potential to positively influence commitment, motivation and performance but only to the extent that it is integrated within a coherent package of HRM strategies. Training is most likely to have a positive impact on motivation, performance and commitment when it is linked to promotion, rewards, future employment prospects and the chance to use the skills developed during training while in the job.

Stop and reflect

Consider a recent training programme that you undertook? Were the objectives of the programme clearly understood? Do you consider the training effective and useful? How might you support your staff in identifying their learning and development needs?

Conclusion to Chapter 3

The first section of this chapter provided an introduction to the concept of human resource management and an overview of the move from personnel management to HRM. The methods an organisation chooses to allocate responsibility for the discharge of human resource functions will be determined by a large number of factors, including the skills and competencies of its line managers, the complexity of its needs, its size and its traditional practices. Nevertheless, since the mid-1980s, a clear trend has emerged for restructuring human resource functions away from personnel departments and towards line managers. This trend places new demands on line managers to become familiar with human resource issues and practices.

However, there remains considerable disagreement about many aspects of HRM. Indeed, there is not an agreed, single definition of HRM that holds for all situations. A working definition that distinguishes it from traditional practices of personnel management can be produced, but evidence for its existence in practice is mixed. There is concern among some that the HRM phenomenon is merely a labelling of a series of piecemeal changes that lack the coherence of the 'model' prescribed in academic and practitioner texts. In other words, practice tends to differ significantly from theory.

Even within these prescriptive models, there are distinct and somewhat contradictory approaches. Here it is particularly important to distinguish between 'hard' and 'soft' approaches. Each has a different perspective on the management of the human resource. It is also important to understand the important connections between HRM and wider changes in the organisation of work, and the concept of 'flexibility' is central. However, again there are differing views on the motivations and consequences of these developments.

Having established in the introductory section the terms of discussion concerning HRM, the sections that followed looked in more detail at three key areas of the HR function: organisational entry, managing performance and rewards, and training and development.

The second section of this chapter argued that what has, in the past, been regarded as the traditional personnel duty of recruiting new employees can be analysed more usefully by a framework of analysis known as 'organisational entry'. The process was described as a sequence consisting of four elements: analysis, recruitment, selection and induction. However, as with all management activities, frameworks and checklists can take you only so far, and managing the entry process can never be made completely formulaic. Indeed, it will usually involve some difficult and uncertain choices.

Recruitment and selection are supposed to be driven by rational decision making in finding the 'best' person for the job. However, you should recognise that practices associated with each step of the recruitment and selection process may well fall short of 'objectivity'. For example, there are different ways of viewing the 'ideal' or 'best' candidate. This could be defined in terms of fitting the organisational culture, or in terms of job specific expertise, or in terms of the likelihood of staying with the organisation. Indeed, the ways in which the profiles of ideal candidates are drawn may be influenced by decisions that reflect the recruiter's values and preferences. Research has suggested that the process of drawing up the profile of the 'ideal candidate' can be rather subjective and mysterious and that this process often reproduces senior managers' self-image (e.g. Van Zwanenberg and Wilkinson, 1993).

Moreover, the selection methods that are typically used in organisations to select candidates, such as the interview, have limited predictive validity and reliability; methods that provide for more accurate evaluation, such as assessment centres, while increasingly popular, tend to be expensive and therefore only accessible to larger organisations that can afford them.

The second section ended with an examination of the organisational exit. Given the increased uncertainty that characterises employment in the twenty-first century, managing organisational exit is an important part of the human resource process. Exit from organisations can take different forms, but recognising the reasons employees leave a company is an important method of monitoring employee relations.

The third section of this chapter examined performance management as a vital aspect of HRM. Performance management is not simply a way of ensuring that standards of work are met, but is also central to motivating workers, identifying training needs and instilling higher levels of commitment in employees. The control loop as a useful way of thinking about managing performance was examined. The control loop involves three main stages: setting specific targets; monitoring the extent to which individuals fulfil these targets; and taking corrective action if necessary. Nevertheless, all stages of this process are not without problems and, at worst, can be regarded as little more than 'box ticking' exercises or sources of organisational conflict.

Performance Related Payment systems were also examined. There is evidence that organisations are using reward systems as a way of facilitating organisational, cultural and strategic change in pursuing the emphasis on quality, flexibility and commitment that is central to HRM philosophy. However, connecting pay with performance can also be problematic. By rewarding the achievement of measurable and short-term goals, it may undermine group cooperation and longer-term commitment. In addition, because of financial constraints, high performers may not receive much more than poor performers and may have their commitment to the organisation weakened rather than increased. Finally, the scope for perceived injustice and bias in the appraisal process may also weaken commitment. These issues will be even more sensitive when levels of pay are involved.

Above all, however, the attitude of the workforce is vital to the success of such payment systems. The most effective way of changing a payment system is to involve, in its design and introduction, representatives of all those who will be affected. Once a payment system has been established, it is important to maintain it and monitor how it is working – changing it if necessary. In particular, it is important to establish procedures for dealing with any problems – for example, if a person feels his or her pay has been assessed incorrectly.

The final section of this chapter highlighted the centrality of training and development to the philosophy of HRM. If HRM is to be something more than managerial rhetoric, then employees must be treated as a 'resource' rather than a cost or commodity. In the so-called 'knowledge economy', this becomes even more important. This implies investment, and training and development are the prime forms of investment organisations can make in human resources. Therefore, the identification of training needs and the formulation of training programmes to meet these needs are of vital importance, as are development opportunities. However, you should also appreciate the many difficulties of evaluating training and development provision.

This section also tried to show how training and development can be integrated into everyday work activities. Ideally it is a continuous process, with no definite end point. Increasingly, organisations are attempting to formulate policies in order to stimulate, manage and find sufficient resources for staff development as an essential element of their efforts to improve performance and effectiveness, and to maximise the opportunities for all. This final section should have helped you consider how you might approach the subject of training and development so that you can recognise other people's needs (as well as your own) and make effective provision for them.

Conclusion to the book

This book has given you the opportunity to learn about the nature of organisations and managing people within organisations. At this stage, we hope you have begun to appreciate how crucially important knowledge and experience of organisations is to being an effective manager. You have looked at how organisations have identified ways to differentiate themselves from others, through structure and design of the organisation. The focus of this book has been on understanding what happens inside organisations, and you have learned how organisations respond to fulfil their needs through people by creating the right internal environment. This leaves as a question to consider in future study, 'How do organisations respond to the external environment?'

The book has given you the opportunity to explore many different approaches to organisational literature that offer guides to how you are managed or manage others. This insight into how managers deal with everyday tasks of planning, leading, organising and controlling should equip you with the right tools to become a successful manager. The challenge, however, is to recognise the choices that are open to a manager in designing or modifying particular organisational arrangements, such as definition of jobs, centralisation, broader or narrower spans of control, single or dual reporting lines, and functional versus other groupings of staff. By applying course concepts and frameworks to workplaces and organisations that you know, you have had practical opportunities to test out how you can use these theories, but we hope you have also had an opportunity to grow as a manager. Finally, we hope you have found this book interesting and thought-provoking.

Glossary

360-degree feedback

An approach to performance appraisal which seeks feedback from different people who work with or come into contact with the individual employee in the work context. Feedback can be provided by superiors, peers, subordinates and customers. This is in contrast to traditional performance appraisal where employees only receive feedback from their managers.

Blind spot

When other group members know things about an individual that the individual does not realise him or herself.

Bureaucracy

One of three ideal models of organisational structure introduced by Max Weber (1864–1920), which defines bureaucratic organisations as hierarchical, governed by rules that regulate conduct, and as having a division of labour based on specialisation.

Control loop

(See Book 1.)

Cognitive tests

Assess attributes such as intelligence, special ability or numerical ability; they have been found to have a relatively high predictive validity; however, some have questioned the extent to which they add to the information that could be obtained from simply looking at academic qualifications.

Collective bargaining

Negotiation of pay and working conditions by an organised body of employees.

Content theories of motivation

Content theories focus on human needs and their satisfaction; 'content' in this context refers to those 'contents' within us that drive or push us (see Kornberger et al., 2008). Content theories include Maslow's hierarchy of needs, ERG theory, Theory X/Theory Y, Herzberg's dual-factor theory.

Convergence and divergence

The convergence–divergence debate in international management and human resource management revolves around whether HRM practices should be the same anywhere (convergent) or adapted according to the cultural setting in which they are practised (divergent).

Customer care

Is an approach to training and development that involves putting systems in place to maximise customers' satisfaction. This often includes rigorous training of front-facing staff such, as reception and sales, staff but also involves making all members of staff aware of the importance of customer satisfaction and the part they play in it.

Differentiation

Segmenting the organisation into sub-systems, each of which tends to develop particular attributes in response to the particular demands posed by its relevant external environment.

Dual-factor theory

Herzberg's theory of two needs – hygiene factors, which involve working conditions and can trigger dissatisfaction, and motivator factors, which originate from the nature of the job itself and can create job satisfaction.

Employment relationship

The legal link between employers and employees.

Expectancy

The degree to which increased effort is perceived to lead to increased job performance; an element of expectancy theory (along with instrumentality and the valence).

Feedback

One of the two key dimensions (the other being risk) in Deal and Kennedy's model of organisational culture (1982). By 'feedback' Deal and Kennedy do not mean just bonuses, promotions and pats on the back. They use the term much more broadly to refer to knowledge of results. An organisation's culture is distinguished by the speed of feedback received, combined with the degree of risk associated with its activities.

Groupthink

Term coined by Irving Janis, who was intrigued by how teams arrive at devastating decisions by ignoring evidence that might suggest that what they are planning to do or have done is ill-advised.

Hard and soft HRM

A distinction made by Storey (1989). The hard form focuses on the cost of human 'resources' and on headcounts. The soft aspect focuses on 'human' aspects such as communication and motivation.

Hawthorne Effect

Refers to a noted tendency wher by some workers respond to the amount of attention they are given, making them feel valued, rather than to the physical working conditions. It is derived from experiments conducted by George Elton Mayo between 1927 and 1933 at the Hawthorne works of Western Electric. Mayo was studying the relation between the amount of light given and productivity but instead found that the productivity increased in any case due to the researchers' presence, highlighting the important of recognition or concern.

Hidden agendas

Things that an individual wants or expects from a group that the group does not know about.

Hofstede's cultural difference model

A model which maps national cultural differences along five dimensions: power distance; individualism/collectivism; masculinity/femininity; uncertainty avoidance; and Confucian/dynamism.

Homeostasis

(See Book 1.)

Human resource management (HRM)

This term has tended to replace the term 'personnel management'. The change of term highlights the way in which employees are viewed as a critical resource for the success of a business and to signify that responsibility for their motivation and success resides with line managers rather than being the sole responsibility of the personnel department.

Industrial tribunals

Introduced in 1964 in the UK, these have powers to hear cases of unfair dismissal, discrimination and other cases relating to contravention of statutory rights.

Instrumentality

The degree to which improved job performance is perceived to lead to desired outcomes; an element of expectancy theory (along with expectancy and the valence).

Job design

The way in which different tasks are put together to make up complete jobs.

Job enrichment

An idea that was developed by the American psychologist Frederick Herzberg in the 1950s. This strives to motivate employees by giving them the opportunity to use the whole range of their abilities in doing their jobs.

Job rotation

An approach to management development where an individual is moved through a schedule of assignments in different departments or sections of an organisation in order to get exposure to the entire operation and to make contacts and share knowledge across functional boundaries.

Learning organisation

A term that gained broad recognition through Senge's book *The Fifth Discipline* (1990), which suggests that a learning organisation values, and derives competitive advantage from, continuing learning, both individual and collective.

Maintenance functions

Within groups, these functions help to maintain the morale and harmony of a group and create an atmosphere in which people feel they can work together productively. In part this is about trying to meet people's needs for inclusion, control, affection and respect.

Maslow's hierarchy of needs

A content theory of motivation which states that motivation stems from the satisfaction of needs, which are arranged in a hierarchy. Lower-level needs must be satisfied before higher-level needs, and once a need is satisfied it ceases to be a motivator.

Matrix-structure

The structure organised around a multiple command system. In such a structure an employee will have two managers: the line manager of the department or division they work for, and the manager of a particular project they are currently involved with. Such projects may also include some or all of the organisation's departmental areas.

Metaphors

Metaphors are rich sources of information about organisations. They are usually based on implicit images, attitudes or beliefs that persuade us to see, understand and imagine situations in partial ways. It is worth noting that metaphors create insight; but they can also distort.

Organisational culture

This term is used to help define the modes of behaviour that are appropriate in an organisation. Just as in a society, or a particular country, different organisations have different 'customs'. Often these are unwritten and unspoken, and new employees learn what is appropriate in a particular organisation's culture over time through socialisation, seeing what others do and listening to how certain actions are viewed by others.

Paradigm

A world view underlying the theories and methodology of a subject or specific area of study.

Performance related pay (PRP)

An individual financial reward in the form of increases to basic pay or cash bonuses that are awarded after meeting agreed objectives, for example, sales targets or customer satisfaction, etc.

Personality tests

Assess individuals against a model of underlying personality factors. Many personality tests are available, with different levels of predictive validity.

Process theories of motivation

Process theories were introduced because it was felt that content theories did not sufficiently explain why people are motivated to behave in certain ways and because to answer such questions it is necessary to consider what processes are involved in motivation. Process theories include equity theory, expectancy theory, goal-setting theory.

Psychological contract

A term coined by Edgar Schein to denote what employees expect from employers, in terms of both pay and of how they will be developed. This unwritten contract also includes an employer's expectations about the loyalty and diligence of the people who work for them.

Rational

Based on or in accordance with reason or logic.

Risk

One of the two key dimensions (the other being feedback) in Deal and Kennedy's model of organisational culture (1982). An organisation's culture is distinguished by the degree of risk associated with its activities, combined with the speed of feedback received.

Scapegoating

The practice of singling out one person or group practice for unmerited blame. The scapegoat is symbolically made to take the blame for the faults of the wider organisation or community.

Self-actualisation

Part of Maslow's hierarchy of needs; see 'Maslow's hierarchy of needs' above. This is seen as the ultimate motivational goal, only achievable once other needs have been met.

Task functions

Within groups, these include ensuring that the group shares a common understanding of the task in hand, problem solving, initiating structures to enable the task to be attained, and controlling the activities of a group to achieve its goal. The specific task functions that are needed will vary according to the nature of the task.

Theory X

One of two different sets of managerial assumptions about people (the other being Theory Y) as hypothesised by McGregor. Theory X assumes that managers are responsible for directing and organising people and that otherwise people are passive.

Theory Y

One of two different sets of managerial assumptions about people (the other being Theory X) as hypothesised by McGregor. Theory Y assumes that management is responsible for organising the elements of productive enterprise, that people are not essentially passive and that management should thus enable people to achieve their goals in a self-directed manner.

Training needs analysis (TNA)

Training and learning needs analysis is a systematic means of checking and recording the skills, talent and capabilities of the organisation. It provides a framework for the gathering of data to find out where there are gaps in the existing skills, knowledge and attitudes of employees and identifying training and development needs and opportunities. This is sometimes conducted in conjunction with performance appraisal.

Total quality management (TQM)

A management approach for long-term success that involves all sectors of the organisation to focus on achieving customer satisfaction. This concept is associated with the work of W. Edwards Deming.

Valence

The valence is the attractiveness of the outcomes to be obtained from increased job performance (for example, increased pay, less chance of being dismissed, the intrinsic satisfaction of doing a good job); an element of expectancy theory (along with instrumentality and expectancy).

References

Adams, J.S. (1963) 'Towards an understanding of inequity', *The Journal of Abnormal and Social Psychology*, vol. 67, no. 5, pp. 422-436.

Alderfer, C.P. (1972) *Existence, Relatedness and Growth*, New York, Free Press.

Alvesson, M. (2002) *Understanding Organizational Culture*, London, Sage.

Antonacopoulou, E. (2001) 'The paradoxical nature of the relationship between training and learning', *Journal of Management Studies*, vol. 38, no. 3, pp. 327–50.

Atkinson, J. (1984) 'Manpower strategies for flexible organisations', *Personnel Management*, vol. 16, no. 8, pp. 28–31.

Becker, G. (1975) *Human Capital: Theoretical and Empirical Analysis*, Chicago, IL, University of Chicago Press.

Belbin, R.M. (1981) *Management Teams: Why They Succeed or Fail*, London, Butterworth-Heinemann.

Belbin, R.M. (1993) *Management Teams: Why They Succeed or Fail*, London, Heinemann.

Berens, L.V., Ernst, L.K. and Smith, M.A. (2004) *Quick Guide to the 16 Personality Types and Teams: Applying Team Essentials to Create Effective Teams*, Telos Publications.

Berger, L.A. and Berger, D.R. (2004) *The Talent Management Handbook*, New York, McGraw-Hill.

Blake, R. and Mouton, J. (1964) *The Managerial Grid*, Houston, TX Gulf Publishing Company.

Bloisi, W., Cook, C.W. and Hunsaker, P.L. (2006) *Management and Organizational Behaviour*, Berkshire, McGraw-Hill.

Bone, J. (2006) '"The longest day": "flexible" contracts, performance-related pay and risk shifting in the UK direct selling sector', *Work, Employment & Society*, vol. 20, no.1, pp. 109–27.

Burrell, G. and Morgan, G. (1979) *Sociological Paradigms and Organizational Analysis*, London, Heinemann.

Camuffo, A., Romano P. and Vinelli A. (2001) 'Back to the future: Benetton transforms its global network', *MIT Sloan Management Review*, vol. 43, issue 1, pp. 46–52.

Castells, M. (2000) *The Information Age*, Oxford, Blackwell.

Clegg, S., Kornberger, M. and Pitsis, T. (2005) *Managing and Organizations: An Introduction to Theory and Practice*, London, Sage.

Coates, G. (2000) 'Experiencing performance appraisal in a trust hospital', *Electronic Journal of Sociology*, vol. 5, no. 1 [online], www.sociology.org/content/vol005.001/coates.html (accessed 20 June 2010).

Crowther, D. and Green, M. (2004) *Organisational Theory*, London, CIPD.

Daft, R.L. (2000) *Management*, Orlando, FL, Harcourt.

Daft, R.L. (2006) *The New Era of Management* (int.ed), London, Thomson.

Davis, S.M. (1984) *Managing Corporate Culture*, New York, Ballinger.

Dawson, S. (1986) *Analysing organisations*, Basingstoke, Macmillan.

Deal, T.E. and Kennedy, A.A. (1982) *Corporate Cultures: The Rites and Rituals of Corporate Life*, Harmondsworth, Penguin.

Department for Children, Schools and Families (DCSF) (2003) 'Boosting skills, productivity and employment', DCSF [online], www.dcsf.gov.uk/pns/DisplayPN.cgi?pn_id=2003_0047 (accessed 15 June 2010).

Department for Trade and Industry (2002) 'Work–life balance' website, DTI, now archived [online], http://webarchive.nationalarchives.gov.uk/+/164.36.164.20/work-lifebalance/index.html (accessed 15 June 2010).

Doyle, M. (2001) 'Management development' in Beardwell, I. and Holden, L. (eds) *Human Resource Management: A Contemporary Perspective*, (3rd edn), London, Pitman.

Duarte, D.L. and Snyder, N.T. (2006) *Mastering Virtual Teams: Strategies, Tools, and Techniques that Succeed*, (3rd edn), San Francisco, CA, Jossey-Bass.

Esser, J.K. and Lindoerfer, J.S. (1989) 'Groupthink and the Space Shuttle Challenger accident: toward a quantitative case analysis', *Journal of Behavioural Decision Making*, vol. 2, no. 1 pp. 167–77.

Etzioni, A. (1988) *The Moral Dimension*, New York, The Free Press.

Feldman, M. (1991) 'The meaning of ambiguity: Learning from stories and metaphors', in Frost, P.J. et al. (eds), *Reframing Organizational Culture*, Newbury Park, Sage.

Felstead, A., Fuller, A., Jewson, N., Kakavelakis, K. and Unwin, L. (2007) 'Grooving to the same tune? Learning, training and productive systems in the aerobics studio', *Work, Employment & Society*, vol.21, no. 2 pp. 189–208.

Fincham, R. and Rhodes, P. (2005) *Principles of Organisational Behaviour,* (4th edn), Oxford, Oxford University Press.

Fitchard, K. (2009) 'Creating culture', *Connected Planet*, 1 July [online], http://connectedplanetonline.com/global/nsn-creating-culture-0701/index.html (accessed 20 May 2010).

Foley, S. (2010) 'Toyoda: "Sometimes we find defects - in our cars and ourselves", *The Independent*, 25 February, [online] http://www.independent.co.uk/news/business/news/toyoda-sometimes-we-find-defects-ndash-in-our-cars-and-ourselves-1909810.html (Accessed 5 April 2010).

Foucault, M. (1979) Discipline and Punish: The Birth of the Prison, London, Allen Lane.

Fowler, A. (1996) *Employee Induction: A Good Start*, London, Institute of Personnel and Development.

Franke, R.H., Hofstede, G., and Bond, M.H. (1991) 'Cultural roots of economic performance: A research note', *Strategic Management Journal*, vol. 12, no. S1, pp. 165-174.

Gabriel, Y. (1999) *Organizations in Depth*, London, Sage.

Garsten, C. (1999) 'Betwixt and between: temporary employees as liminal subjects in flexible organisation', *Organisation Studies*, vol. 20 no. 4, pp. 601–17.

Gibson, O. (2010) 'Red Knights confirm plans for Manchester United bid', *The Guardian*, 2 March [online], www.guardian.co.uk/football/2010/mar/02/red-knights-manchester-united (accessed 10 June 2010).

Govindarajan, V. and Gupta, A. (2001) 'Building an effective global business team', *MIT Sloan Management Review*, vol. 42, no. 4, pp. 63–71.

Grey, C. (2005) *A Very Short, Fairly Interesting and Reasonably Cheap Book About Studying Organizations*, London, Sage.

Grint, K. (1993) 'What's wrong with performance appraisal? A critique and a suggestion' *Human Resource Management Journal*, vol. 3 no. 3, pp. 61–77.

Guest, D. (1987) 'Human resource management and industrial relations', *Journal of Management Studies*, vol. 24, no. 5, pp. 503–21.

Halsall, R. (2008) 'From "business culture" to "brand state": conceptions of nation and culture in business literature on cultural difference', *Culture and Organization,* vol. 14, issue 1 (March), pp. 15–30.

Handy, C.B. (1976/1999) *Understanding Organizations*, (4th edn), Harmondsworth, Penguin Books.

Harrison, R. (1972) 'Understanding your organization's character', *Harvard Business Review*, vol. 50, no. 3, pp. 119-128.

Harvey, J., Carter, S. and Mudimu, G. (2000) 'A comparison of work values and motives among Zimbabwean and British managers', *Personnel Review*, vol. 29 no. 6, pp. 723–42.

Hatch, M.J. (1997) *Organization Theory*, Oxford, Oxford University Press.

Henderson, F., Anderson, N. and Rick, S. (1994) 'Future competency profiling: validating and redesigning the ICL graduate assessment centre', *Personnel Review*, vol. 24 no. 3, pp. 18–31.

Herriot, P. (1992) 'Selection: the two subcultures', *European Work and Organisational Psychologist*, vol. 2, pp. 129–40.

Herriot, P. (1993) 'A paradigm bursting at the seams', *Journal of Organisational Behavior*, vol. 14, pp. 371–5.

Herzberg, F. (1968/2003) 'One more time: how do you motivate employees?' in *Harvard Business Review on Motivating People*, Boston, MA, Harvard Business School Press.

Heyes, J. and Stuart, M. (1996) 'Does training matter? employee experiences and attitudes', *Human Resource Management Journal*, vol. 6 no. 3, pp. 7–21.

Hofstede, G. (1983) 'The cultural relativity of organizational practices and theories', *Journal of International Business Studies*, vol. 14, pp. 75-89.

Hofstede, G. (1994) *Cultures and Organizations: Software of the Mind*, London, Fontana.

Hofstede, G. (2001) *Culture's Consequences*, (2nd edn), Thousand Oaks, CA, Sage.

Hofstede, G. and Bond, M.H. (1988) 'The Confucius connection: From cultural roots to economic growth', *Organizational Dynamics*, vol. 16, no. 4, pp. 5-21.

Holden, L. (2001) 'Human resource development: the organisation and the national framework' in Beardwell, I. and Holden, L. (eds) *Human Resource Management: A Contemporary Perspective,* (3rd edn), London, Pitman.

Holden, N. (2002) *Cross-cultural Management: A Knowledge Management Perspective*, Harlow, Pearson Educational.

Iles, P. and Salaman, P. (1995) 'Recruitment, selection and assessment' in Storey, J. (ed.) *HRM: A Critical Text*, London, Routledge.

Jackson, N. and Carter, P. (2000) *Rethinking Organizational Behaviour*, Harlow, Financial Times Prentice Hall.

Jacob, N. (2005) 'Cross-cultural investigations: emerging concepts', *Journal of Change Management*, vol. 18, issue 5, pp. 514–28.

Jacoby, S.M. (2005) *The Embedded Corporation: Corporate Governance and Employment Relations in Japan and the United States*, Princeton, NJ, Princeton University Press.

Janis, I.L. (1972) *Victims of Groupthink*, Boston, MA, Houghton Mifflin.

Kakabadse, A., Ludlow, R. and Vinnicombe, S. (1988) *Working in Organisations*, Harmondsworth, Penguin.

Kanter, R.M. (1984) *The Change Masters*, London, Allen and Unwin.

Knight, P.J. (2006) *Small, Short Duration Technical Team Dynamics*, Defense Acquisition University Press.

Korczynski, M. (2005) 'Skills in service work: an overview', *Human Resource Management Journal,* vol. 15 no. 2, pp. 3–14.

Kornberger, M., Clegg, S. and Pitsis, T. (2008) *Managing and Organizations: An Introduction to Theory and Practice*, (2nd edn), London, Sage.

Lambert, S. (2008) 'Passing the buck: labour flexibility practices that transfers risk onto hourly workers', *Human Relations*, vol. 61 no. 9, pp. 1203–27.

Lawley, J. (2001) 'Metaphors of organisation – part 1', *Effective Consulting*, vol. 1, no. 4 (September) [online], www.cleanlanguage.co.uk/articles/articles/19/1/Metaphors-of-Organisation-part-1/Page1.html (accessed 22 May 2010).

Lawrence, P. and Nohria, N. (2002) *Drives: How Human Nature Shapes Our Choices*, San Francisco, CA, Jossey-Bass.

Lawrence, P.R. and Lorsch, J.W. (1967) *Organization and Environment*, Cambridge, MA, Harvard University Press.

Legge, K. (2005) *Human Resource Management: Rhetorics and Realities*, London, Macmillan Business.

Lewis, P. (2001) 'Reward management' in Redman, T. and Wilkinson, A. (eds) *Contemporary Human Resource Management*, Harlow, Pearson, pp. 98–127.

Linstead, S.A. and Grafton-Small, R. (1992) 'On reading organizational culture', *Organizational Studies*, vol. 13, issue 3, pp. 331–55.

Locke, E.A. and Latham, G.P. (1969) 'Goal-setting – A technique that works', *Organisational Dynamics*,vol. 8, Autumn, pp. 68–80.

Locke, E.A., Shaw, K.N., Saari, L.M. and Latham, G.P. (1981) 'Goal setting and task performance 1969–1981', *Psychological Bulletin*, vol. 90, pp. 125–52.

Louis, M. (1985) 'An investigator's guide to workplace culture', in Frost, P. et al. (eds), *Organizational Culture*, Newbury Park, Sage.

Macleod, D. and Clarke, N. (2009) 'Engaging for success: enhancing performance through employer engagement. A report to Government' [online], www.bis.gov.uk/files/file52215.pdf (accessed 15 June 2010).

March, C. (2009) *Business Organisation for Construction*, London, Taylor and Francis.

Marchington, M. and Wilkinson, A. (2006) *Human resource Management at Work: People Management and Development*, (3rd edn), London, CIPD.

Martin, J. (2002) *Organizational Culture: Mapping the Terrain*, London, Sage.

Maslow, A.H. (1943) 'A theory of human motivation', *Psychological Review*, vol. 50, pp. 370–96.

Maslow, A.H. (1970) *Motivation and Personality*, New York, Harper & Row.

McGivern, G. and Ferlie, E. (2007) 'Playing tick-box games: interrelating defences in professional appraisal', *Human Relations*, vol. 60 no. 9, pp. 1361–85.

McGregor, D. (1960) *The Human Side of Enterprise*, New York, McGraw-Hill Higher Education.

McGregor, D. (1989) 'The human side of enterprise' in Leavitt, H., Pondy, L. and Boje, D. (eds) *Readings in Managerial Psychology*, (4th edn), Chicago, IL, University of Chicago Press, pp. 314–24.

McSweeney, B. (2002) 'Hofstede's model of national cultural differences and their consequences: a triumph of faith – a failure of analysis', *Human Relations*, vol. 55, issue 1, pp. 89–106.

Mintzberg, H. and Waters, J.A. (1985) 'Of strategies deliberate and emergent', *Strategic Management Journal*, vol. 6, pp. 257–72.

Molander, C. (1986) *Management Development*, Lund, Sweden: Chartwell-Bratt.

Morgan, G. (1986) *Images of Organization*, London, Sage.

Morgan, G. (1989) *Creative Organization Theory: A Resource Book*, London, Sage.

Morgan, G. (2007) *Images of Organization*, (updated edn), London, Sage.

Mullins, L.J. (2008) *Management and Organisational Behaviour*, (6th edn), London, Financial Times Prentice Hall.

Myers, S. (2010) *MTR-i™ Team Role articles* [online] http://www. teamtechnology.co.uk/mtr-i.html, (Accessed 18 July 2010).

Newell, S. and Shackleton, V. (2001) 'Selection and assessment as an interactive decision-action process' in Redman, T. and Wilkinson, A. (eds) *Contemporary HRM: Text and Cases*, Harlow, Pearson, pp. 24–56.

Ngai, P. and Smith, C. (2007) 'Putting transnational labour process in its place: the dormitory labour regime in post-socialist China', *Work, Employment & Society*, vol. 21 no. 1, pp. 27–45.

Orozco, D. (1995) 'Orientation' in Smiley, J. and Kenison, K. (eds) *The Best American Short Stories*, Houghton Mifflin.

Parsloe, P. (1981) *Social Services Area Teams*, London, Allen and Unwin.

Paton, R.C. (1991) 'The social economy; value-based organizations in the wider society' in Batsleer, J., Cornforth, C. and Paton, R. (eds) *Issues in Voluntary and Non-profit Management*, Wokingham, Addison Wesley.

Peters, T.J. and Waterman, R.H. (1982) *In Search of Excellence*, New York, Harper & Row.

Proctor, S. and Currie, G. (1999) 'The role of the personnel function: roles, perceptions and processes in an NHS trust', *International Journal of Human Resource Management*, vol. 10, no. 6, pp. 1077–91.

Pugh, D. (ed.) (2007) *Organization Theory: Selected Classic Readings*, (5th edn), London, Penguin.

Pugh, D. and Hickson, D.J. (1989) *Writers on Organizations*, (4th edn), London, Penguin.

Pugh, D. and Hickson, D.J. (2007) *Writers on Organizations*, (6th rev. edn), London, Penguin.

Randell, G. (1994) 'Employee appraisal' in Sisson, K. (ed.) *Personnel Management*, (2nd edn), Oxford, Blackwell.

Rarick, C. and Nickerson, I. (2008) 'Combining classification models for comprehensive understanding of national culture: metaphorical analysis and value judgements applied to Burmese cultural assessment', *Journal of Organizational Culture, Communications and Conflict*, vol. 12, no. 2, pp. 9–19.

Redman, T. (2005) 'Performance appraisal' in Redman, T. and Wilkinson, A. (eds) *Contemporary Human Resource Management*, Harlow, Pearson.

Redman, T. and Wilkinson, A. (eds) (2005) *Contemporary Human Resource Management*, Harlow, Pearson.

Renwick, D. and Gennard, J. (2001) 'Grievance and discipline' in Redman, T. and Wilkinson, A. (eds) *Contemporary HRM: Text and Cases*, Harlow, Pearson, pp. 168–91.

Robbins, S. (2001) 'Culture as communication', *Harvard Business Review*, vol. 4, issue 8, pp. 1–4.

Roberts, I. (1997) 'Remuneration and rewards' in Beardwell, I. and Holden, L. (eds) *Human Resource Management*, (2nd edn), London, Pitman.

Roberts, J. (2007) 'Motivation and the self' in Knights, D. and Wilmott, H., *Introducing Organizational Behaviour and Management*, Thomson, London.

Rollinson, D. (2008) *Organizational Behaviour and Analysis: An Integrated Approach*, (4th edn), London, Pearson Education Ltd.

Rowley, C. and Bae, J. (2002) 'Globalization and transformation of human resource management in South Korea', *International Journal of Human Resource Management*, vol. 14, no. 4, pp. 17–33.

Rowley, C., Benson, J., and Warner, M. (2004) 'Towards an Asian model of human resource management? A comparative analysis of China, Japan and South Korea', *International Journal of Human Resource Management*, vol. 13, no. 3, pp. 522–49.

Sathe, V. (1983) 'Implications of corporate culture: A manager's guide to action', *Organizational Dynamics*, vol. 12, no. 2, pp. 5-23.

Schein, E. (1980) *Organisational Pyschology*, (3rd edn), London, Prentice-Hall.

Schein, E. (1992) *Organizational Culture and Leadership*, San Francisco, CA, Jossey-Bass.

Scullion, H. (1995) 'International human resource management' in Storey, J. (ed.) *Human Resource Management: A Critical Text*, London, Routledge.

Sengupta, K. (2009) '"Lamentable" failures led to Nimrod crash that killed 14: inquiry names 10 people to blame for worst military disaster since Falklands War', *The Independent*, 29 October [online], www.independent.co.uk/news/uk/home-news/lamentable-failures-led-to-nimrod-crash-that-killed-14-1811133.html (accessed 15 June 2010).

Sergiovanni, T. J. and Corbally, J. E. (eds) (1986) *Leadership and Organizational Culture*, Urbana, IL, University of Illinois Press.

Sivakumar, K. and Nakata, C. (2001) 'The stampede toward Hofstede's framework: avoiding the sample design pit in cross-cultural research', *Journal of International Business,* vol. 32, issue 3, pp. 555–74.

Smircich, L. (1983) 'Concepts of culture and organizational analysis', *Administrative Science Quarterly*, September, pp. 339–59.

Smith, P. (2002) 'Culture's consequences: something old and something new', *Human Relations*, vol. 55, issue 1, pp. 119–35.

Stanton, A. (1989) *Invitation to Self-management*, London, Dab Hand Press.

Storey, J. (1995) *Human Resource Management: A Critical Text*, London, Routledge.

Stredwick, J. and Ellis, S. (1998) *Flexible Working Practices: Techniques and Innovations*, London, CIPD.

The Sunday Times (2010) 'The Sunday Times 100 best companies 2010' [online], www.business.timesonline.co.uk/tol/business/career_and_jobs/best_100_companies/best_100_tables/ (accessed 26 August 2010).

Surman, E. (2002) 'Dialectics of dualisms: the symbolic importance of the home/work divide', *Ephemera*, vol. 2, no. 3, pp. 209–23.

Thompson, P. and McHugh, D. (2002) *Work Organisations: A Critical Introduction*, (3rd edn), Basingstoke, Macmillan.

Thornhill, A. and Saunders, M.N.K. (1998) 'What if line managers don't realise they're responsible for HR? Lessons from an organisation experiencing rapid change', *Personnel Review*, vol. 27, no. 6, pp. 460–76.

Trice, H.M. and Beyer, J.M. (1984) 'Studying organizational cultures through rites and rituals', *Academy of Management Review*, vol. 9, issue 4, pp. 653–69.

Trompenaars, F. and Hampden-Turner, C. (2003) *Riding the Waves of Culture: Understanding Cultural Diversity in Business*, London, Nicholas Brealey.

Tuckman, B.W. (1965) 'Development sequence in small groups', *Psychological Bulletin*, vol. 63, pp. 384–99.

Tuckman, B.W. and Jensen, M.A.C. (1977) 'Stages of small group development revisited', *Group and Organizational Studies*, vol. 2, pp. 419-427.

Tyson, S. and York, R. (1996) *Human Resource Management*, (3rd edn), Oxford, Butterworth-Heinemann.

Van Zwanenberg, N. and Wilkinson, L. (1993) 'The person specification – a problem masquerading as a solution?', *Personnel Review*, vol. 22, no. 7, pp. 54–65.

Vroom, V.H. (1964) *Work and Motivation*, New York, Wiley.

Weber (1952) 'The essentials of bureaucratic organization: An ideal-type construction', in Merton, R.K. et al. (eds) *Reader in Bureaucracy*, Glencoe.

Weick, K.E. (1995) *Sensemaking in organizations*, London, Sage.

Willmott, H. (2002) 'Strength is ignorance; slavery is freedom: managing culture in modern organizations' in Clegg, S.R. (ed.) *Central Currents in*

Organization Studies II: Contemporary trends, Volume 7, London, Sage; originally published in *Journal of Management Studies*, vol. 30, pp. 515–82.

Wong, C. et al. (1997) 'Management training in small and medium-sized enterprises: methodological and conceptual issues', *International Journal of Human Resource Management*, vol. 8, no. 1, pp. 44–65.

Zeitz, G. (1980) 'Interorganizational dialectics', *Administrative Science Quarterly*, vol. 25, no. 1, pp. 72–88.

Acknowledgements

Grateful acknowledgement is made to the following sources:

Cover

Cover image: © iStockphoto.com;

Figures

Figure 1.4: From: Introducing Organisation behaviour and management, Knights, D. and Willmott, H. © 2007, Thomson Learning. Reproduced by permission of Cengage Learning;

Figure 1.6: Deal, T. and Kennedy, A. (1982) *Corporate Cultures: The Rites and Rituals of Corporate Life*, Perseus Books Publishing, L.L.C.;

Figure 2.1: Maslow A. (1970) 'Hierarchy of needs'. Adapted from Maslow, 1970;

Figure 2.2: Moorhead, G. and Griffin, R.W. (1995) *Organizational Behaviour*, 4th edn. Houghton Mifflin Company;

Figure 3.1: Atkinson, J. (1984) 'Manpower strategies for flexible organisations', *Personnel Management*, 16/8, People Management;

Illustrations

Page 9: The Domestic System, courtesy of Chris Trueman;

Page 9: Production of Nokia E75 in Salo factory, Finland. Image courtesy of Nokia. Copyright © 2010 Nokia;

Page 24: Charlie Chaplin (1936) *Modern Times*. © Everett Collection / Rex Features;

Page 24: Charlie Chaplin (1936) *Modern Times*. © SNAP / Rex Features;

Page 40: © iStockphoto.com/Ales Kramer;

Page 41: Oxfam Be Humankind. With permission from Oxfam GB;

Page 43: © Francis Vachon/Alamy; 26 August 2010. Page 1 of 2;

Page 44: © Keso/flickr;

Page 44: © Neil Tingle/Alamy;

Page 47: 'Think'. Reprint Courtesy of International Business Machines Corporation, © International Business Machines Corporation;

Tables

Table 1.1: Morgan, G. (2007) 'Chapter 6, Interests, conflict, and power: organizations as political systems', *Images of Organisation*. © Sage Publications Inc. Books

Text

Pages 13, 22 to 23, 27 to 28, 31 to 32: Pugh, D.S. and Hickson, D.J. (2007) *Writers in Organisations*, 6th edn, pp. 59–60, 7–8, 243–6, 124–5, copyright © D.S. Pugh and D.J. Hickson. Reproduced by permission of Penguin Books Ltd;

Pages 17 to 18: Camuffo, A., Romano, P. and Vinelli, A. (2001) 'Back to the Future: Benetton transforms its global network', *MIT Sloan Management Review*, Vol. 43, Issue 1. © 2010 from MIT Sloan Management Review/ Massachusetts Institute of Technology. All rights reserved. Distributed by Tribune Media Services;

Pages 57 to 58: Fitchard, K. (2009) 'Creating Culture', www.connectedplanetonline.com, July 1. Penton Publishing Inc.;

Page 90: Myers, S. The MTR-I Team Roles;